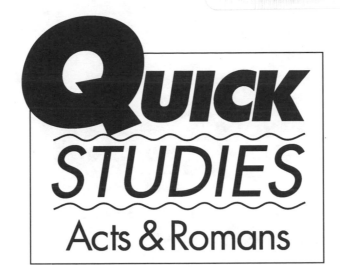

Cook Ministry Resources
a division of Cook Communications Ministries
Colorado Springs, Colorado/Paris, Ontario

The following authors and editors contributed to this volume:

Stan Campbell
John Duckworth
Rick Thompson
Jim Townsend, Ph.D.

Quick Studies
Acts and Romans

Cook Ministry Resources
a division of Cook Communications Ministries
4050 Lee Vance View; Colorado Springs, CO 80918-7100
Cable address: DCCOOK
Designed by Bill Paetzold
Cover illustrations by Steve Björkman
Inside illustrations by Jack DesRocher and Paul Turnbaugh
Printed in U.S.A.

ISBN: 0-7814-0026-0

ACTS

ROMANS

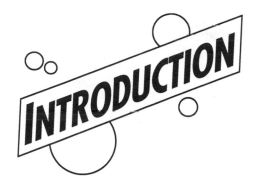

Quick Questions about Quick Studies

We've made *Quick Studies* as self-explanatory as possible, so you can dive in and start using them right away. But just in case you were wondering . . .

When should I use *Quick Studies*?

Whenever you want high school or junior high kids to explore the Bible face-to-face and absorb it into their lives. We've kept the openers active and the discussion questions creative, so you can use *Quick Studies* with confidence in Sunday school, midweek youth Bible study, small groups, even youth group meetings and retreats.

What's so quick about *Quick Studies*?

They're designed to save you preparation time. The session plans are compact, for quick reading. There aren't a lot of materials to gather, either (you'll need Bibles, pencils and paper, copies of the reproducible sheets, and sometimes a few other items). Yet *Quick Studies* are *real* Bible studies, with plenty of thought-provoking discussion and life application.

How are these different from other youth Bible studies?

We like to think *Quick Studies* are . . .

• *Irresistible.* You already know most kids don't jump at the chance to fill in a bunch of blanks in a boring study guide. So we used creative, reproducible sheets and *active* activities to draw kids into Scripture.

• *Involving.* You need discussion *starters*, not discussion *stoppers*. We avoided dull "yes or no" questions and included lots of thought-provokers that should get your group members talking about important issues. And we didn't forget suggested *answers* to most of the tougher questions, which should make things easier for you.

• *Inductive.* Many Bible studies try to force-feed kids a single "aim" and ignore other points Scripture is trying to make. *Quick Studies* let kids discover a variety of key principles in a passage.

• *Influential.* It's not enough to know what the Bible says. Every session includes a step designed to help kids decide what to do *personally* with vital points from the chapter.

When do kids read the passages covered?

That's up to you. If your group is into homework, assign the passages in advance. If not, take time to read the Scripture together after the "Opening Act" step that kicks off each session. There are dozens of ways to read a passage—with volunteers taking turns, or with a narrator and actors "performing" a scene, or with kids underlining points as they read silently, or with you reading as the author and kids listening as the original audience, or with small groups paraphrasing as they read . . .

What if I want to cover more—or less—than a chapter in a session?

Quick Studies are flexible. Each 45- to 60-minute session covers a chapter of the New Testament, but you can adjust the speed to fit your group. To cover more than one chapter in a session, just pick the points you want to emphasize and drop the activities, questions, and reproducible sheets you don't need. To cover less than a chapter, you may need to add a few questions and spend more time discussing the "So What?" application step in detail.

Do I have to cover a whole New Testament book?

No. Each session stands alone. Use sessions one at a time if you want to, or mix and match books in any order you choose. No matter how you use them, *Quick Studies* are likely to help your group see Bible study in a whole new light.

John Duckworth, Series Editor

ACTS 1

Final Exit

The Book of Acts, a "sequel" to Luke's Gospel, begins with some of the last words of Jesus and His ascension into heaven. We are also told of the violent death of Judas and his replacement among the disciples. The "Christian community" at this time consists of a small band of believers numbering about 120.

(Needed: Two or more toasters; bread; peanut butter; jelly)

Bring in two or more toasters (the kind where the toast pops up). Have kids guess which toaster will finish first. Start the toasters at the same time (on similar settings) and let the cheering begin! Let those who guessed correctly eat the toast with peanut butter and jelly (make more pieces, if necessary). Use this to lead into a discussion of waiting.

DATE I USED THIS SESSION _____ GROUP I USED IT WITH _____

NOTES FOR NEXT TIME_____

_____

_____

1. When have you had the hardest time waiting for something?

2. Luke, the author of the Book of Acts, explains to his friend Theophilus that Jesus had instructed the disciples to wait. Precisely what were their instructions (vss. 1-5)? (They were to remain in Jerusalem and wait for the outpouring of the Holy Spirit.) **What do you suppose they were thinking and feeling? What questions might they have had?**

3. Do you or your friends ever wonder about the certainty of Jesus' resurrection? In what ways? What proofs did Luke provide that Jesus' resurrection hadn't been a hoax? (Jesus had made several appearances—one in front of more than 500 people [I Corinthians 15:3-7] and another where He ate [Luke 24:42, 43. See also Acts 1:4]. These appearances took place over a 40-day period, in different places, to different people, and the people were still around to testify to that fact. So surely Jesus' appearances were genuine.)

4. Apparently some of the disciples were still hoping to be charter members of the kingdom of Israel they thought Jesus was to establish on earth, but Jesus wanted them to focus their attention elsewhere. What were they to do (vss. 6-8)? (They were to wait for the power provided by the Holy Spirit, and then be witnesses for Him [Jesus]. Note the progression—starting in Jerusalem and extending to the ends of the earth.)

5. In fact, these were Jesus' last words on earth, which would indicate that this was an important message. What happened then to confirm this (vss. 9-11)? (Jesus ascended into heaven, and immediately two angels began to challenge the disciples to prepare for His return.)

6. If you had been one of the disciples, what would you have done to pass the time while you waited? Compare this with what the disciples actually did (vss. 12-14). (They "constantly" joined together in prayer.) **Is this activity something that brings *you* closer to others? Explain.**

7. By this time the disciples were beginning to piece together the facts of Jesus' resurrection with what He had tried to tell them before He died and with what Scripture said would happen. For example, they discovered that Psalm 69:25 and 109:8 could refer to their situation with Judas. By the way, what had happened to Judas (vss. 15-19)? (According to Matthew 27:5, Judas hanged himself. Here it says he fell headlong and his body burst open. This could have occurred when the body was cut down. Others suggest that the word translated "hanged" in Matthew could also mean "impaled.")

8. The disciples decided to replace Judas, and at this time there were 120 believers to choose from (vs. 15). **What do you think about how they decided to do this** (vss. 20-26)? (They narrowed it down to their top two candidates, prayed, and cast lots, which was a common practice at this time. It suggests that they trusted God's choice. However, this is the last time casting lots is mentioned in the Bible. After this, the Holy Spirit would be their guide.)

9. Do you have any methods you regularly use to make hard decisions?

10. If you were one of the members of the group at this time, how do you think you would feel? (Disappointed because Jesus was no longer there; confused; doubtful that things could continue without the leadership of Jesus; excited about what was to happen, etc.)

Someone once said, "The only person who likes change is a wet baby." Even though change in life is inevitable, we often resist it. In Acts 1, the disciples were facing some drastic changes. The reproducible sheet, "As the World Changes," helps group members think through several situations where someone must cope with change. How might a relationship with God help these people better cope with the changes they're facing? After discussing these hypothetical situations, talk through some of the changes people in your group are actually facing. How are they handling them? Talk about the pros and cons of change and the resources we have as Christians to cope with change.

As the World Changes

Things change, but life goes on. How do you think the characters in these daytime dramas should cope with the changes in their lives?

❷ ALL MY TEACHERS.

Brock's teacher has been sick a lot lately, and the regular substitute, Mrs. ("Genghis") Conway has been filling in. Since she's only a sub, Brock and his classmates haven't exactly gone out of their way to be polite. And since she's on the serious side, Brock figures he can run her out and get someone more fun. He's been the ringleader in devising new tactics: answering to other people's names, hiding her attendance book, providing wrong information when she asks what they've been studying, and so forth. In today's episode, however, she announces that the regular teacher is too ill to continue the year, so she is now the permanent teacher. She looks straight at Brock as she says, "There will need to be some changes made."
Stay tuned: What does Brock do?

❺ ANOTHER MOVE.

As a junior in her midwest school, Veronica is class president and the life of every party. She can't wait until her senior year. But then her mom announces that she has a job opportunity in California that's just too prime to pass up. They quickly sell their house, say their good-byes, and move. When Veronica gets there, she admits that she could get used to the climate and the beach. But then she has her first day of school, and she's met with stares not unlike the ones she and her old friends used to save for Ricky Ratzenbaumer, "King Dweeb of the Universe." As she goes through the first week of school, she just can't seem to connect with anyone. The classes seem harder, the people seem colder, and her mom is spending a lot of extra hours in her new job.
Don't touch that dial: How does Veronica respond to all these changes?

❼ GENERATIONAL HOSPITAL.

Natasha and her teenage granddaughter, Ingrid, are best friends—no two people have ever been closer. They do *everything* together. They're always trying new things and taking new risks (traveling, rafting, hang gliding—you name it). But after a routine visit to the doctor, Natasha is in shock, announcing that she has been diagnosed with an incurable illness. In the months that follow, Natasha gets weaker, loses her hair, and cannot participate in many of the normal things she used to—not to mention the more exciting ones.
Don't go away: How does Ingrid react to these changes in her relationship?

Evangelism Explosion

In response to Jesus' previous instructions, the disciples are waiting in Jerusalem. And true to His promise, the Holy Spirit arrives in a miraculous display seen as tongues of fire that rest on each person. As a result, the believers are able to speak different languages and tell what God has done—in the language of every visitor to Jerusalem. Peter explains this phenomenon to the gathering crowd. About three thousand people become believers, and the church begins to take shape.

Ask for volunteers in groups of three at a time. One volunteer should act as a visitor from the faraway country of Absurdo. This person, of course, should speak Absurdian. The second volunteer is a translator, who understands Absurdian and converts it to English. The third volunteer can play himself or herself, meeting this visitor for the first time. Conduct a "conversation" for a while, as the first volunteer invents a language, the second one appears to understand it and translate, and the third one asks questions. Have fun with this, but be sure to deal with question #1 in the "Q & A" section before moving into the text. We should not take lightly the work of the Holy Spirit.

DATE I USED THIS SESSION _____ GROUP I USED IT WITH _____

NOTES FOR NEXT TIME _____

_____

_____

1. What problems or challenges do different languages create for us? What do you think is the best way to communicate with people who speak other languages?

2. Jesus had instructed the disciples to wait in Jerusalem for the coming of the Holy Spirit. What do you suppose they were expecting? What actually happened when the Holy Spirit arrived (vss. 2-4)? (Accompanied by the sound of a rushing wind, the visible manifestation of something like "tongues of fire" rested on each of the apostles who were then instantly able to speak other languages.)

3. What was the result of this event (vss. 5-13)? (People from every nation heard their language being spoken by unschooled Galileans. Many were amazed and perplexed. Others were skeptical, thinking the disciples were drunk.)

4. How are people today skeptical of God's work in the world? How do they explain away things like Creation and answered prayer?

5. Peter said that he and the others weren't drunk. He tied this event to the prophecy in Joel 2:28-32. According to this Scripture, what would be the result of this event (vss. 14-21)? (Everyone who calls on the name of the Lord will be saved.)

6. Not long before this, Peter had been lurking in the shadows, afraid to admit that he even knew Jesus. But now he speaks with a new courage. Read through his message (vss. 22-36) and see if he says anything that *you* might be reluctant to say to a curious crowd. (He boldly proclaims the facts about the life, death, and resurrection of Jesus, tying them to Old Testament Scripture. And he didn't hold back in stating that it was these people—the Jewish leaders—who put Him to death [vs. 23], and that God had now made Jesus "both Lord and Christ" [vs. 36]. These were courageous words for a onetime fisherman to direct to a large crowd.)

7. How did the crowd respond to Peter's words (vss. 37-41)? (The people were "cut to the heart," and wanted to know what to do. Many repented and were baptized.) **Do you think you would have been one of the repentant crowd, or are you more likely to have tried to defend your previous actions? Why?**

8. **In one day the number of believers in Jesus went from about 120** (Acts 1:15) **to approximately 3,120** (vs. 41). **There had been plenty of confusion and conflicts when it was just Jesus and the twelve disciples. What would you expect from a crowd of more than 3,000 people coming together and trying to get along?** (Probably more conflicts and confusion.) **What actually happened as the people began to interact as a group?** (Eating and praying together, miracles performed by the apostles, sharing, praising God, and the spread of the Gospel message.)

9. **What do you think made such a difference in how people were relating?** (The Holy Spirit unites believers. Jesus had promised that the Spirit would guide people in repentance and truth [John 16:7-15].)

10. **Do you feel that you know as much about the work of the Holy Spirit as you do about God the Father and Jesus? Explain.** (One function of the Spirit is to bring glory to Jesus [John 16:13, 14]. Yet we should not be in the dark as to the attributes of this third part of the Trinity.)

The reproducible sheet, "That's the Spirit," will have your group members look at the changes that were made as a result of the Holy Spirit coming to Jerusalem. The effects of the Holy Spirit were obvious. Can we say the same today? After you discuss their responses, spend some time as a group trying to put together a plan that would help you all become "one in the Spirit."

THAT'S THE SPIRIT

YOUTH RETREAT

In the days just prior to Jesus' crucifixion, the future of Christianity didn't look too strong. The disciples, the people who were closest to Jesus, were sleeping, betraying, denying, and hiding. The Jewish people were shouting, "Crucify Him!" It's hard to imagine that this group of "losers" would ever amount to much without their leader.

But there was one factor that hadn't yet been considered. Jesus promised to send the Holy Spirit after He returned to heaven. And what a difference the Spirit made! Those cowardly disciples started standing up and preaching to huge crowds of people. Some of the people who had demanded Jesus' death now repented and received Him as their Savior. And the previous arguments that had taken place as to who was greatest dissolved into a lifestyle of unity and compassion.

Now that the Holy Spirit has come into the world, has He come into your group? On the following checklist, taken from Acts 2, see how well you think your group performs these functions. (1 = Lousy; 10 = Wonderful.)

Devotion to teaching (learning)	1	2	3	4	5	6	7	8	9	10
Devotion to fellowship	1	2	3	4	5	6	7	8	9	10
Eating together	1	2	3	4	5	6	7	8	9	10
Devotion to prayer	1	2	3	4	5	6	7	8	9	10
Full of wonder at the things God is doing	1	2	3	4	5	6	7	8	9	10
Witnessing wonders and miraculous signs	1	2	3	4	5	6	7	8	9	10
Searching out common interests	1	2	3	4	5	6	7	8	9	10
Selling possessions to help those of the group who are in need	1	2	3	4	5	6	7	8	9	10
Offering regular praise to God	1	2	3	4	5	6	7	8	9	10
Enjoying each other's company	1	2	3	4	5	6	7	8	9	10
Bringing in new people regularly	1	2	3	4	5	6	7	8	9	10

One thing we can do to improve this group:

ACTS 3

The Bouncing Beggar

At the temple gate Peter and John encounter a beggar who has been disabled since birth. The beggar asks for money, but gets healed instead. The man's healing causes quite a stir among people in the temple courts, and Peter seizes the opportunity to speak to the crowd about the Gospel of Jesus Christ.

(Needed: Food item or money)

Hold a begging contest. Bring in some type of food that your kids love (if not food, money would work) and give individuals a chance to beg for it. Whoever can do the most convincing job of begging should get the prize. The issue of begging follows in the questions and the text.

DATE I USED THIS SESSION _____ GROUP I USED IT WITH _____

NOTES FOR NEXT TIME _____

_____

_____

1. Can you think of a time when you wanted something really, really badly, but you received something else instead that turned out to be even better? (Not being able to travel with friends during the summer, but finding a great job and making lots of money instead; having your eye on the "perfect" sweater, but receiving an even better one as a gift, etc.)

2. Peter and John had an encounter with a beggar (vss. 1-3) who thought he knew what he wanted. What is your first impression when you see someone begging? How do you think this man felt?

3. What did the beggar want? Why? (He wanted money because he had been disabled from birth and had no way to make a living.) Do you think this was a reasonable request? (During this time, before there were any governmental or private social agencies, the man's options would have been very limited.)

4. What do you think of the way Peter and John responded to this man (vss. 4, 5)? (They wanted to establish eye contact with him.) Then what did they do (vss. 6, 7)? (Rather than give the man money, Peter used the power of God to heal him.)

5. How did the man respond to their unanticipated gift (vs. 8)? (He made good use of his legs for the first time in his life—not only walking, but jumping as well. And though he followed Peter and John, he praised God.)

6. How did people find out about this miracle (vss. 9, 10)? (They recognized the man and were amazed at the change. [This should be true whenever God works in someone's life. The "before" and "after" should be so significant that other people sit up and take notice.])

7. How did other people know it was Peter and John who had helped the man (vs. 11)? (The thankful beggar continued to hold on to them.)

At this point, read through Peter's speech to the crowd

(vss. 11-26). Hand out the reproducible sheet, "Spur-of-the-Moment Sermons," and have kids fill out the top half. They are to give a title to Peter's sermon, jot down his main point, identify any Scripture texts he used, and develop a brief outline of his remarks. (Some possible answers: Title—"God Did It!" Main point—It was God's power that healed the man; you can experience God's power by repenting and having faith in the name of Jesus. Scripture texts—Isaiah 52:13—53:8 [vs. 18]; Deuteronomy 18:15, 18, 19 [vss. 22, 23]; Genesis 22:18 [vs. 25]. Outline—vss. 12-14 = recent events; vss. 15-18 = God's plan; vss. 19-26 = your choice.)

8. **How was Peter's "sermon" in this chapter similar to the one he gave in Acts 2?** (Both contain accusations that the religious leaders put Jesus to death, Old Testament references, and an outline of God's plan for the salvation of mankind including Christ's resurrection and the need for repentance.)

9. **Have you ever experienced a "time of refreshing" after telling God you were sorry for committing a sin** (vs. 19)? **Is confession a regular part of your spiritual life?** (Some people try to justify all their "little" sins. Others hope to keep them hidden. Some people just don't care.)

10. **What was the good news for these people listening to Peter** (vss. 22-26)? (The prophecies of the prophets were now coming to pass. Moses, Samuel, and many others had foretold the coming of Jesus and the benefits that would be received. Now, these people were the first "heirs of the prophets and of the covenant God made.")

Fill out the bottom portion of the reproducible sheet, "Spur-of-the-Moment Sermons." This time kids are to outline a sermon they would give if called upon to do so at a moment's notice. Ask for volunteers to share their titles, main points, Scripture texts (if they can think of any), and outlines. Stress the importance of including personal experience. Don't force this; be sensitive to those who have not yet established a strong relationship with Jesus. Encourage these people to write down any questions they might have about Jesus.

SPUR OF~THE MOMENT SERMONS

Peter was prepared to preach at the drop of a hat (or the jumping of a beggar). Read his speech in Acts 3:12-26.

Give a title to his "sermon":

_____

What's his main point?

_____

What references does he make to the Old Testament?
(It's okay if you can't quote chapter and verse, just list what he talks about.)

_____

How would you outline his remarks?_____

_____

_____

Now it's your turn. Suppose you're sitting in church and the preacher suddenly looks a little green. He's obviously sick. He motions to you to come to the front of the church to present the sermon. You think, "No problem, I can do that." While the congregation sings one more song, jot down a few details about your sermon in the space below. (Oh, cool, everybody's looking at you.)

Title:_____

Main point:_____

Scripture text(s):_____

Outline: _____

_____

_____

_____

Bold Is Beautiful

After healing the disabled man (Acts 3), Peter and John are seized and jailed overnight by the Jewish religious leaders. But Peter speaks up strongly, and the healed man is in attendance so there can be no question of the miracle that has taken place. Peter and John are released; the believers rejoice, thank God, and continue to share their possessions with each other.

(Needed: Scissors; small prize [optional])

Prior to meeting, make copies of the reproducible sheet, "I Witness." Cut the sheets along the dotted line. Give each kid a copy of the picture and two minutes to study it. After two minutes, collect the pictures and hand out the questions. See who can get the most correct answers. (Answers: [1] 3:12 P.M.; [2] First National Federal Savings Interstate Bank; [3] at the corner of Elm St. and Grove Ave.; [4] three; [5] baseball cap, smiley face T-shirt, long pants, and no shoes; [6] Mickey Mouse ears; [7] 2-door; [8] X CON; [9] we don't know, even though there's a gun outside the bank; [10] car was illegally parked.) Award your winner(s) a small prize if you want. In this chapter we see Peter and John witnessing for Christ— they can't help speaking about what they've seen and heard (vs. 20).

DATE I USED THIS SESSION _____ GROUP I USED IT WITH _____

NOTES FOR NEXT TIME _____

_____

_____

1. Have you done something with the best of intentions, which really pleased one person (or group of people), but upset another person (or group) instead?

2. In Acts 3, Peter and John had healed a disabled beggar, instructing him in the name of Jesus to walk. The man was overjoyed. But what were the consequences of this action (vss. 1-3)? **Why?** (Peter and John had upset the religious leaders, especially the Sadducees, who taught that there was no resurrection. As a result, Peter and John were tossed into jail overnight.)

3. Do you think it was worth the effort: a night in prison to heal one person? Why? (See verse 4. Many people believed in Jesus because of this miracle. The last count of believers had been about three thousand [2:41]. Now it was up to five thousand.)

4. Peter had talked about Jesus boldly a couple of times before. This time he was addressing some of the community leaders who had the authority to keep him in jail or let him go. Would you have changed your message? Did he (vss. 5-12)? (No way. He couldn't have made it clearer that the people there were responsible for crucifying Jesus, that God had raised Him from the dead, and that because Jesus now lives again, He is the one source of salvation.)

5. As the Jewish religious leaders watched and listened, what struck them in addition to the message (vs. 13)? (Peter and John had not been formally trained in religion—or public speaking, for that matter. They were "unschooled, ordinary men." And it's interesting to note that at this point the religious leaders realized that these men had traveled around with Jesus.)

6. Based on this, what do you need before you can tell others about Jesus? (Primarily, a personal relationship with Him and a sensitivity to the leading of the Holy Spirit. Deep theological training, a knowledge of Bible facts, memorization of long passages, and such are nice as well—but not requirements for being a witness.)

7. The healed man was standing right there, and there was little the religious leaders could do. So they just instructed Peter and John to stop talking about Jesus. **Why didn't the apostles take this advice** (vss. 14-22)? (They explained that all they were doing was attesting to the things they personally had witnessed, and that they had the responsibility to follow God rather than men.)

8. **What was the effect of the release of Peter and John on the new group of people who believed in Jesus** (vss. 23-31)? (They immediately united in prayer, thanked God, and prayed for further boldness. It had to be encouraging to see that they served a God who would stand by them in trying times.)

9. **The believers continued to share what they had with each other, and no one was needy** (vss. 32-35). **But one particular giver was singled out at this point. What was his name, and what was his nickname** (vss. 36, 37)? (His name was Joseph, but the apostles called him Barnabas ["Son of Encouragement"].) **What's the last thing you've done to encourage someone?**

10. How would you like to have been part of this group of believers? What would you have liked about it? What would have been a big adjustment for you?

Talk about what it means to be bold about your faith in the following situations: at school; at work; at a party; at home. Use questions like the following to continue your discussion: **When do you find it hardest to be bold about your faith? Why is it sometimes hard to be bold? What keeps us from being bolder? How could a shy person be bold in his or her faith? Is it ever possible to be too bold about your beliefs?**

WIT**I**NESS

You're standing outside the bank when it's robbed! Study this picture carefully for two minutes. You'll soon be questioned by the police.

- -
P O L I C E   Q U E S T I O N S

1. What time did the robbery take place?

2. What was the name of the bank?

3. Where was the bank located?

4. How many bags of money were stolen?

5. What was the robber wearing?

6. What was the accomplice wearing?

7. Was the robber getting into a 2-door or 4-door car?

8. What was the license number of the car?

9. Was anybody inside the bank shot?

10. What other crime was being committed?

Drop Dead

Deceit threatens the growing group of people who believe in Jesus, as Ananias and Sapphira lie about a gift they have given and are struck dead because of their actions. Yet the group continues to flourish as the apostles continue a healing and teaching ministry. Persecution continues, but God protects them in wonderful ways. Meanwhile, a wise Pharisee named Gamaliel offers sound advice in regard to this new "cult."

(Needed: Colored markers; sample greeting cards [optional])

Give everyone a supply of paper and colored markers. Have kids create two greeting cards. The first should be insincere; the second should be brutally honest. You might want to have a few cards on hand to inspire creativity. Let kids work together if they want to. Here's an example of an insincere card: "Roses are red, violets are blue/It's your birthday and I'm thinking of you/On the day you were born all wars came to an end/Now everyone's everyone else's best friend." Here's a "brutally honest" version: "Roses are red, violets are blue/I felt I had to buy this card for you/The only reason I'm sending it your way/Is because I want one back on my birthday." After sharing your cards, lead into a discussion about lying.

DATE I USED THIS SESSION _____ GROUP I USED IT WITH _____

NOTES FOR NEXT TIME _____

_____

_____

Q&A

1. What are some common things that people lie about? Why is lying so common?

2. During the formation of the church, two people found out just how dangerous lying can be. The early church was made up of people who were sharing, giving, and becoming as close to each other as possible (Acts 4:32-37). There was no place for deceit, yet what did Ananias and Sapphira do (vss. 1, 2)? (They sold some of their property, kept a little for themselves, and gave the rest to the apostles. But they made it seem that they were giving the whole amount.)

3. As lies go, how severe do you think this one was (on a scale of 1 to 10)? Can you think of any lies you've told that seem just as bad, or worse? (Don't force anyone to share here; simply give kids a moment to reflect on their own lives.)

4. Why do you think they received such a harsh punishment? Wouldn't a strong warning have been enough? (Since the church was just beginning to take shape, people were starting to watch the believers very closely. The love, joy, and peace they displayed were attractive elements, yet people were not to forget that the Holy Spirit was responsible for these things. God was in control and would not be mocked. If Ananias and Sapphira went unpunished, people might logically think that God didn't know, or looked the other way, when sins were committed.)

5. What effect did the deaths of Ananias and Sapphira have on the church (vss. 11-14)? (It seems that from that point on, only people who were serious about commitment joined the group.)

6. How could people tell God was at work (vss. 15, 16)? (They were healed of all kinds of diseases. The apostles displayed God's power in much the same way Jesus had.)

7. Those poor religious leaders . . . they thought if they got rid of Jesus their problems would go away. Now there were *lots* of people displaying the power Jesus had used.

So what did the religious leaders do (vss. 17, 18)? (They tossed all the apostles in jail.)

8. But God has a wonderful way of making the bad intentions of some people turn out for our good. So what happened (vss. 19-26)? (An angel freed them, and they immediately went out to the temple to teach. The jail was still locked. The guards were still there. But God's people were out doing their job.)

9. When they finally confronted the Jewish leaders, the apostles were as bold as ever. And the Jewish council wanted to have them killed (vss. 27-33). **But at the advice of Gamaliel, one of their respected leaders, they didn't. What was Gamaliel's advice** (vss. 34-39)? **How does it apply to cults today?** (He reminded the Sanhedrin of two previous attempted revolts that fizzled out because the leader had died. With Jesus gone, he reasoned, so would this new movement—if it were based on man-made principles and commitments, that is. If it were truly of God, on the other hand, the Sanhedrin could not stop it anyway. So it is with some new "religious" movements today. Given time, the leader gets bored, arrested, or dies, and the whole system falls apart. But after two thousand years, Christianity is still going strong.)

10. What was the result of this encounter between the apostles and the Sanhedrin (vss. 40-42)? (The apostles were flogged and sternly warned not to speak in the name of Jesus again. Then they went right out and kept doing what God had told them to do.)

The apostles repeatedly refused to obey the authorities as they continued to publicly proclaim the Good News. Use the reproducible sheet, "Obey—Yea or Nay?" to discuss similar situations that might take place today. For some guidance on what to do in these situations, check out Romans 13:1-7. Some of these situations are more clear-cut than others. Simply use them to get discussion going. Talk about similar situations your kids might be faced with in their own lives.

OBEY—
Yea or Nay?

In Acts 5:29, we find Peter and the other apostles saying some famous words: "We must obey God rather than men." But the Bible also says, "Remind the people to be subject to rulers and authorities, to be obedient, to be ready to do whatever is good" (Titus 3:1). What gives? When are we supposed to obey God, and when are we supposed to obey other people in authority over us?

What would you do in each of these situations?

1 Your school has a policy that no classrooms are to be used by religious organizations. Some Christians at school are trying to organize a prayer meeting there anyway. They want you to come.

2 Your youth group wants to see a certain video, and you agreed to pick it up at the video store. Unfortunately, it won't be available the night you want it, but you could make an illegal copy a couple days before. You figure that since it's for use at church, it's probably not wrong.

3 You work at a grocery store after school. One day your boss asks you to change the expiration date on some products, so that they don't have to be taken off the shelf. You feel a bit uneasy about it.

4 You have a chance to travel to a foreign country on a choir tour. This country applies very high taxes to Bibles and religious books in order to discourage people from bringing them in. But since you're traveling with a large group, it would be possible to smuggle several Bibles into the country without the officials knowing it. In fact, some of the local churches where you'll be performing have asked you to do so.

5 Sometimes your youth leader takes you to public places in order to hand out tracts and talk to people about Jesus. One day, you decide to witness at the mall. You didn't realize that the mall has a policy prohibiting "solicitation," and that's what they consider evangelism to be. While you're talking to someone, a security guard asks you to leave.

6 As an assignment for a class, your teacher asks you to read something that makes fun of Christianity. It's also full of profanity. You're not sure if you should read it, but you also don't want to risk getting a bad grade.

ACTS 6

Meals on Wheels

With the growth of the early church, problems begin to arise. People are being added on a regular basis, and some of them begin to feel overlooked. The apostles cannot attend to all the needs of the people, and decide they must focus on the spiritual development of the new church. Therefore, they appoint seven people to help them with day-to-day duties. But as the effectiveness of the church grows, so does opposition from the traditional religious leaders.

(Needed: Paper plates)

Give each group member a paper plate to balance on his/her head. Then challenge kids to perform various tasks without the plates falling. (Possible tasks: sit on the floor and stand up; catch a ball; turn around three times, etc.) Make the tasks increasingly difficult, until no one is able to keep the plate balanced. In this chapter, the leaders of the early church were having difficulty balancing the many things they had to do.

DATE I USED THIS SESSION _____ GROUP I USED IT WITH _____

NOTES FOR NEXT TIME_____

_____

_____

(Needed: Paper to serve as a menu; a book; nail clippers; toothbrush)

1. **When was the last time you were so busy that you just about went crazy trying to get everything done? How did you get that way? What happens when you have too much to do?** (Discuss how sometimes things get done sloppily, or not at all.)

2. **How is this skit sort of like the situation faced by the leaders of the early church? How is it different?** (The leaders were too busy to be able to effectively wait on tables. But in Acts, they were busy doing worthwhile things like praying and spreading the Word. As they tried to take care of the needs of the people, they were accused of providing food for the local Jewish widows [the Hebraic Jews], but not for the ones from outside that immediate area [the Grecian Jews].)

3. **What did they propose to remedy the situation** (vss. 2-4)**?** (While the apostles continued to take care of the spiritual needs of the church, they appointed seven others to tend to people's material needs. Note that both types of service are important and require people full of the Spirit and wisdom.)

4. **What happened as a result of this division of labor** (vss. 5-7)**?** (Because of the willing service of both groups, the number of believers continued to grow rapidly.)

5. **Even many of the priests were beginning to believe in Jesus. But not all. There was still jealousy on the part of some of the Jewish religious leaders. And rather than go up against the apostles or the church as a whole, they selected one of the appointed leaders, Stephen, to oppose. Why do you think they singled him out** (vs. 8)**?** (Stephen was very effective in showing God's grace and power, which got the people's attention.)

6. **What tactics did the religious leaders use to oppose Stephen** (vss. 8-11)**?** (First they tried to debate him, but he spoke with wisdom provided by the Holy Spirit. So when that didn't work, they convinced people to accuse him falsely.)

7. Does the treatment of Stephen remind you of anyone else who experienced the same opposition? (It is almost exactly the same way the religious leaders plotted against Jesus.)

8. How did Stephen respond to his arrest and the lies brought against him (vss. 12-15)? ("His face was like the face of an angel." No one could tell that he was even upset or discouraged.)

9. How do you think you would have responded if you had been in the same situation? What's the worst opposition (persecution) you have faced in your own Christian life?

(Needed: paper plates)

Stephen's trial is continued in the next chapter of Acts. Meanwhile, have your group members focus on the content of this chapter—the assignment of people who devoted their skills to meeting people's material needs ("waiting on tables"). Select two actors to perform the skit on the reproducible sheet, "The Dumb Waiter." Make sure the waiter has the necessary props. After the skit, discuss things your group could do that would be like waiting on tables. Perhaps it's delivering meals to a needy family, or helping to clean up the church building. Whose needs in your congregation might be unintentionally overlooked? What could be done to help lighten the load of your church leaders? In the skit, the waiter kept getting distracted from the job at hand. What things might distract us from serving? Choose one specific service project to do together as a group.

THE DUMB WAITER

(Scene opens with customer entering the restaurant. Waiter is sleeping.)

Customer: Excuse me, but I'd like a table.

Waiter: (*Waking up.*) Oh, just a sec. I was catching forty winks. Gotta sleep whenever you can. Know what I mean? (*Stretches and yawns.*) Table for one?

Customer: Please.

Waiter: Right this way. (*Starts jogging over to the table. Continues to jog in place while saying:*) I didn't get a chance to exercise this morning, so I'm trying to get some while I wait on tables. Care to join me?

Customer: No, thanks. How 'bout a menu?

Waiter: No problemo. (*Jogs over and gets a menu and hands it to customer. While customer looks at it, waiter sits down and starts reading a book.*)

Customer: (*Starting to get annoyed.*) Um, aren't you forgetting something?

Waiter: How did you know? I forgot the answer to the third question—it's my homework for history class. Do you know who won the War of 1812?

Customer: No, I meant aren't you forgetting to take my order?

Waiter: Don't have a cow, man. I'll get to it—right after I clip my nails. (*Brings out nail clipper from pocket and starts clipping nails. Waits a little while.*) So, what did you want to order?

Customer: I'll have the daily special.

Waiter: One daily special coming up. I'll turn your order in to the chef— right after I go out and wax my car.

Customer: On second thought, cancel my order. I'm leaving. (*Gets up to leave.*)

Waiter: Um, aren't *you* forgetting something?

Customer: Like what?

Waiter: My tip!

Customer: Sure, I'll give you a tip—if you want to wait on tables, you can't do all the other stuff at the same time.

Waiter: Wow, I never thought of that. Thanks for the tip, man. (*Pulls out toothbrush to brush teeth as customer exits.*)

A Stone's Throw

Stephen, who has been arrested and falsely accused by jealous religious leaders, is on trial. In defense, Stephen recounts the history of Israel and points out how many of God's prophets were misunderstood and persecuted. He ties this directly into his accusers' previous rejection of Jesus. His presentation so infuriates the leaders that they stone him to death.

Form two groups. Give one group a few minutes to write down what they consider the top ten events in world history. Have the other group come up with a list of the top ten most influential people throughout history. Share your lists together. Later on, compare your lists to the events and people that Stephen mentions in his speech.

DATE I USED THIS SESSION _____ GROUP I USED IT WITH _____

NOTES FOR NEXT TIME _____

_____

_____

1. If you were about to be executed, what might you be thinking during your final moments? What might your last words be?

2. In this chapter Stephen has been arrested just because he was doing good things in the name of Jesus. He hadn't hurt anybody, but the religious leaders felt threatened because the number of followers of Jesus was growing rapidly. And in response to the charges, Stephen reminds the "court" of several key figures in Israel's history. (Make a list of some of the people and events that Stephen mentions. Stephen's speech makes for a great Old Testament history lesson!)

• **How had the nation of Israel gotten started in the first place** (vss. 1-8)? (God had led Abraham from the land of Mesopotamia and given him that land as an inheritance. Abraham's great-grandchildren became the twelve tribes of Israel.)

• **What part did Joseph play in Israel's history** (vss. 9-16)? (Joseph, who was sold as a slave to the Egyptians, eventually saved his entire family.)

• **God used another unlikely hero to deliver Israel from the bondage of the Egyptians. Though Moses may not have looked like a hero, how had God prepared him** (vss. 17-36)?

• **What happened to the Israelites when they didn't listen to the leader God had chosen for them** (vss. 37-43)? (For not obeying Moses, they had to wander in the wilderness an additional forty years before entering the promised land. Then, as a result of continual disobedience over a long period of time, God allowed them to be taken captive by their enemies.)

• **God had provided a portable Tabernacle for His people as they traveled. When they settled, He had given them specific instructions for how to build a temple. But what were the shortcomings of these worship areas** (vss. 44-50)? (They were symbols. The presence of God was not intended to be confined to a single building.)

3. **After Stephen's history lesson, he turned to current events. What accusations did Stephen level against these people** (vss. 51-53)**?** (They resisted the Holy Spirit, ignored the prophecies concerning Jesus, and murdered God's own Son. Note that Stephen never mentions Jesus by name, but the crowd got his message.)

4. **Though these Jewish leaders could not be reasoned with, Stephen knew he was right. How** (vss. 54-56)**?** (He could see Jesus standing at the right hand of God in heaven.)

5. **Perhaps the religious leaders knew Stephen was right as well. But they were in no mood to admit it. What was the result of the fury that had built up within them** (vss. 57, 58)**?** (They became a screaming mob that dragged Stephen out of the city and stoned him. Note the first mention of Saul [Paul] in this passage.)

6. **Stephen's death is quite an example for us** (vss. 59, 60). **What can we learn from it?** (If our focus is on Jesus, we don't have to feel fear or hatred. Stephen was able to forgive the very ones who were throwing the stones. Compare Stephen's last words to what Jesus said in Luke 23:34.)

We can't control the responses of other people when we tell them things they don't want to hear. But we *can* choose our own responses when people confront us with unpleasant messages. The student sheet, "Grudge Match," asks your group members to give responses to unpleasant statements. If Stephen could forgive strangers even as they struck him with stones, we should be able to forgive people for these types of offenses. At the bottom of the sheet, encourage students to list any grudges they are currently holding against people they know. Spend some time in prayer, asking your students to think of the things they have listed and take steps to let go of the grudges.

GRUDGE
M A T C H

In each of the following situations, check what your response would be (or better yet, write in a more appropriate one).

1 Your little brother informs you that he got grease all over your brand new sweater. You reply:

___ That's okay. Here, borrow my new shirt, too.

___ Don't ever ask to borrow any of my stuff again as long as you live—which, if I have anything to do with it, won't be very long.

___ Other:

2 Your mother just volunteered you to baby-sit in the church nursery, but you had already made plans with your friends. You say:

___ No problemo. I just love little children.

___ If you don't get me out of it, I'll volunteer you to sing the national anthem at our next basketball game.

___ Other:

3 Your teacher accuses you of cheating, since your answers are identical to those of the person sitting next to you. Actually, that person copied your answers. You say:

___ I can see how you'd reach that conclusion and I won't hold it against you. You obviously hold academic integrity in high regard. I'm fortunate to have you for a teacher.

___ You're out of your mind.

___ Other:

4 Your coach blames you for losing the game, even though you did your best. What do you say?

___ I know how you feel. I can tell you care a great deal for my overall character development.

___ I didn't blow the game; you did with your lousy coaching.

___ Other:

5 Your date calls you up at the last minute to tell you he/she can't go out with you tonight because he/she decided to go out with someone else. You've already spent about $50 on tickets, and can't get your money back. How do you respond?

___ Thanks for calling. I hope the two of you have a wonderful time.

___ I didn't want to go out with you anyway. Thanks for sparing me the public humiliation.

___ Other:

List some grudges you're holding at this time, or the people you hold them against:

ACTS 8

The Word Spreads

Due to great persecution against the church in Jerusalem, the apostles spread their ministries throughout Judea and Samaria. As Saul intensifies his efforts to arrest those involved in the new church, Peter and John try to set straight a self-seeking sorcerer, and Philip encounters a confused, but curious, foreign eunuch.

(Needed: A supply of Nerf balls, foam rubber, or sponges)

Form teams. See which team can fit the most Nerf balls, sponges, or pieces of foam rubber into a shoe. Shoes should be turned upside down. Anything that falls out doesn't count. After you declare a winner (or a tie), take the stuff out of the shoe and watch it expand. This is sort of like what happens with the church—sometimes people try to squash it, but it always bounces back. In fact, persecution usually results in growth. This is what is going on in Acts 8.

DATE I USED THIS SESSION _____ GROUP I USED IT WITH _____

NOTES FOR NEXT TIME _____

_____

_____

1. Can you think of something bad that's happened to you that turned into something good?

2. After Jesus returned to heaven and sent the Holy Spirit, the early church grew real fast. But its success and growth had been very threatening to the established religious leaders. They had just stoned Stephen. Now what was their plan (vss. 1-3)? (To organize a full-scale persecution of the church.)

3. Why didn't this plan succeed (vs. 4)? (Instead of focusing all their attention in Jerusalem, the disciples scattered. Of course, they took the message of the Gospel with them wherever they went. It was like trying to stamp out a fire, with the burning embers starting new fires wherever they landed.)

4. When you face difficult times, are you more likely to give up or try harder? Give an example or two.

5. What can we learn about Philip (vss. 5-7)? (Philip was a strong spiritual leader. He used the power of God to cast out evil spirits, heal people, and teach.)

6. The power of God that Philip displayed caught the attention of Simon the Sorcerer. What did Simon learn from Philip (vss. 9-13)? (The power of God had purpose—to heal, to bring comfort, and so forth. Simon had used sorcery as a means to set himself up as someone important. He had people thinking he was divine. But when given a choice, the people quickly believed in Philip's God rather than Simon. And though it says that "Simon himself believed," there will soon be a question as to the extent of his belief.)

7. Philip's work in Samaria had broken new ground. (The Jews and Samaritans had long been enemies of each other.) When news of the Samaritans' acceptance of the Gospel reached the church in Jerusalem, they sent Peter and John to follow up. What did Simon the sorcerer learn from Peter and John (vss. 14-25)? (God's power is not for sale! Anyone who tries to profit selfishly from what God provides can only expect trouble.)

8. Read verses 26-40. **What kind of guy was Philip?** (Courageous; open to God's leading; familiar with Scripture; willing to share his faith, etc.) **If you could ask Philip one question, what would it be?** (Some might want to know how the Spirit spoke to him. Others might be curious about his mysterious disappearance in verse 39.)

9. **What do you suppose the Ethiopian eunuch told people about his experience in the desert?** (Certainly he would have told people about the new life he found in Christ. He might also have mentioned Philip's mysterious disappearance. Note: Philip reappeared about nineteen miles away. He then found his way to Caesarea, where he was twenty years later [Acts 21:8].)

Keep talking about Philip's willingness to follow God's Spirit into an unknown situation. Use the reproducible sheet, "On a Mission from God," to get your group thinking about how likely they would be to follow through on various missions. Continue your discussion with questions like these: **If you told God you were willing to serve Him anywhere, where would you most want to go? Where would you least want to go? How do you think you'd know what God wants you to do? How willing are you to go wherever He wants you to go?**

Philip was given a mission—to "go south to the road—the desert road—that goes down from Jerusalem to Gaza." (Acts 8:26). He followed through, and the rest is history. How likely would you be to follow through on each of these missions?

1. Take two years after high school or college to work as a short-term missionary in central Africa.
  ___ Piece of cake!   ___ I'd think about it.   ___ No way, José!

2. Take two years after high school or college to work as a short-term missionary in Europe.
  ___ Piece of cake!   ___ I'd think about it.   ___ No way, José!

3. Help serve meals in a homeless shelter one night a week.
  ___ Piece of cake!   ___ I'd think about it.   ___ No way, José!

4. Help serve meals in a homeless shelter one night a month.
  ___ Piece of cake!   ___ I'd think about it.   ___ No way, José!

5. Talk to a total stranger about your relationship with Jesus.
  ___ Piece of cake!   ___ I'd think about it.   ___ No way, José!

6. Talk to a close friend or family member about your relationship with Jesus.
  ___ Piece of cake!   ___ I'd think about it.   ___ No way, José!

7. Talk to someone who's very curious about having a relationship with Jesus.
  ___ Piece of cake!   ___ I'd think about it.   ___ No way, José!

8. Spend a summer volunteering to paint houses in your hometown.
  ___ Piece of cake!   ___ I'd think about it.   ___ No way, José!

9. Spend a summer teaching Bible school at a Native American Indian reservation.
  ___ Piece of cake!   ___ I'd think about it.   ___ No way, José!

10. Spend a summer on a beach evangelism trip to Hawaii.
  ___ Piece of cake!   ___ I'd think about it.   ___ No way, José!

ACTS 9

Blinded by the Light

As Saul goes about persecuting members of the new church, he has a personal and undeniable encounter with Jesus. Yet as soon as he begins to state that Jesus is the Son of God, his old peers try to have him killed, and the disciples don't trust him. Meanwhile, Peter continues to perform amazing miracles.

(Needed: Unpopped popcorn; corn popper)

Form teams and give a copy of the reproducible quiz, "Odd One Out," to each team. Make sure you cut off the answer key from the bottom of the sheet before you copy it! Announce that the first team to get all the answers right will get some popcorn. When a team thinks it has all the right answers, one person from that team should bring it to you for your approval. If all answers are correct, announce a winner. If one or more answers are wrong, simply tell the person how many answers are wrong—not which ones are wrong. Keep going until one team gets them all right. When finished, explain that in this chapter, people had difficulty identifying Saul as a Christian, and for a while he didn't seem to belong. Award some unpopped popcorn to the winning team. After kids complain, tell them that Saul wasn't "much good" before his conversion, but he sure was afterward. Pop the corn and enjoy it together as you launch into your study.

DATE I USED THIS SESSION _____ GROUP I USED IT WITH _____

NOTES FOR NEXT TIME_____

_____

_____

Q&A

1. Who is someone you know who has changed a lot in attitude or behavior? What caused this change? How did people react to this person after he or she began to be different?

2. The Book of Acts hasn't said much about Saul to this point, though from now on he will be a key character. We know he was young (7:58), opposed to Christianity (8:1), and quite actively involved in stamping out this new movement (8:1-3). **But some changes were about to be made. What caused them** (vss. 1-6)? (As Saul traveled to Damascus to further persecute church members, a bright light from heaven stopped him, and Jesus spoke to him.)

3. Saul was part of a group at the time. **Could the others confirm what had happened to him** (vss. 8, 9)? (They could hear a sound and knew that something had happened, but the message was directed to Saul alone. Obviously, they would notice his changed behavior.) **Can other people confirm your own conversion to Christianity? Explain.**

4. After such a dramatic encounter, how did Saul know he hadn't been hallucinating? (He was blinded and had to be led into Damascus.)

5. Meanwhile, Jesus also appeared to a man named Ananias. **If you had been Ananias, how do you think you would have responded to the Lord's request** (vss. 10-15)? **Why?** (Saul already had a reputation, and had come to town for the sole purpose of arresting Christians [or worse]. It had to be a terrifying proposition to be the first person to walk up to him and say, "So, I hear you're one of us now.")

6. It took a little convincing, but Ananias finally went. **What was the result of this first encounter** (vss. 17-19)? ("Something like scales" fell from Saul's eyes, and he was able to see again.) **When you became a Christian, were you able to "see" anything more clearly than you had previously? If so, explain.**

7. What was the reaction of the Jewish religious leaders to Saul's conversion (vss. 20-26)? (They staked out the city of Damascus, hoping to find and kill him.) **Why do you think they reacted so strongly?** (Saul was an intelligent, well trained, strong person who had been intent on exterminating this new Christian "sect." To have him join their ranks must have been not only embarrassing, but threatening as well.)

8. **Why weren't the Christians glad to see him? Explain.** (Because Saul was smart and had been so ruthless, it was only normal to think that he might be setting a trap. At this point, he had lost the support of his old friends and had not yet made new Christian friends.) **Did you experience any similar problems in transition when you became a Christian?** (It is not unusual to lose some of our old friends when we commit ourselves to Christ.)

9. **So how did Saul "break into" the church group at Jerusalem** (vss. 27-31)**?** (As Ananias had done in Damascus, Barnabas courageously received him and introduced him to the other Christians.)

10. **Peter was still active as well. What kinds of things was he doing to the glory of God** (vss. 32-43)**?** (He healed a man who had been paralyzed for eight years, and he even raised a woman from the dead.)

11. **How do you think Dorcas felt to be brought back to life: (a) happy? (b) disappointed? (c) confused? (d) something else?**

Spend some time discussing your own conversion experiences. Have any group members had dramatic conversions like Paul's? How do those who have grown up in Christian homes describe their conversions? Are there any group members who haven't had a conversion experience, or aren't sure? How can you tell whether or not you've been converted? How could Paul tell?

ODD 1 OUT

One of the items in each of the following lists doesn't belong. Which one is it? The first team to correctly identify all the objects that don't belong wins.

1. a. Happy
   b. Grumpy
   c. Dumbo
   d. Sneezy

2. a. Argon
   b. Helium
   c. Hydrogen
   d. Mercury

3. a. Hosea
   b. Joel
   c. Amos
   d. Jude

4. a. 10
   b. 64
   c. 100
   d. 144

5. a. John
   b. Paul
   c. Steve
   d. George

6. a. Mountain Dew
   b. Seven Up
   c. Coca-Cola Classic
   d. Pepsi

7. a. Thomas Jefferson
   b. Abraham Lincoln
   c. Franklin Pierce
   d. Hubert Humphrey

8. a. Seahawks
   b. Steelers
   c. 49ers
   d. Bears

9. a. Christianity
   b. Buddhism
   c. Islam
   d. Confucianism

10. a. Cantaloupe
    b. Caterpilar
    c. Cinnamon
    d. Corduroy

Answers: (1) c (not one of the seven dwarfs); (2) d (not a gas); (3) d (not an Old Testament book); (4) a (only one that doesn't have an even square root); (5) c (not a first name of one of the Beatles); (6) b (doesn't contain caffeine); (7) d (not a president of the U.S.); (8) a (never won a Super Bowl); (9) a (only one with a living founder); (10) b (only one that is misspelled).

ACTS 10

Peter, Peter, Kosher Eater

Christianity is about to be offered to the Gentiles. God prepares a Gentile named Cornelius to receive the message, and prepares Peter to present it. And sure enough, as the Gentiles respond to Peter's message, they receive the Holy Spirit and are baptized.

(Needed: Blender; assortment of foods listed)

Bring out a blender, some ice cream, and some milk. Tell your group that you're going to make a shake. All those who want some should stand up. If after a while people decide they don't want the shake anymore, they can sit down. Put some ice cream and milk in the blender. Then add some chocolate syrup. Then add a banana (some may sit down at this point). Now let your imagination run wild. Start adding things like pickles, mayonnaise, lemon juice, coffee grounds, and vinegar. Challenge whoever is left standing (if anyone) to drink some of your shake. Explain that Peter probably had much the same disgusted reaction to the sheet full of food in this chapter that your students did to their "shake."

DATE I USED THIS SESSION _____ GROUP I USED IT WITH _____

NOTES FOR NEXT TIME _____

_____

_____

1. Have you ever been to a worship service that's really different from the way we worship in this church? (Perhaps of another religion or denomination.) **What things did that group do differently? How did their worship practices make you feel?**

2. The two big divisions during the early days of the church were between the Jews (descendants of Abraham who lived by the Mosaic law) and the Gentiles (most of whom followed false gods). Since Jesus had been Jewish, that's where Christianity started. But God was ready to spread Christianity to the Gentiles as well. **What kind of person was He preparing to receive the message** (vss. 1-8)? (Cornelius had a good job and was devout, God-fearing, giving, and prayerful.)

3. **Who was God preparing to deliver the truth about Christianity, and how did He prepare him** (vss. 9-16)? (God gave Peter a symbolic vision of "unclean" animals [representing the Gentiles] that had previously been prohibited, but were now acceptable.)

4. What's the most disgusting thing you've ever eaten, or know that some people in other cultures eat? Some of the things in this sheet seemed just as repulsive to Peter. And while Peter was confused at first, God soon began to make the meaning clear. **What did Peter do to make Gentiles feel comfortable mixing with Jews** (vss. 17-23)? (Peter's invitation for his Gentile visitors to stay with him was significant because such intermingling was usually strictly avoided.)

5. Sometimes we get really defensive about what we believe and don't keep an open mind as to what others think. This had been true between the Jews and Gentiles. **Do you think it was true of Cornelius** (vss. 24-26)? (No. Rather, he had too much respect for Peter.) **Was it true of Peter** (vss 27-29)? (No. He, too, was willing to overlook traditional prejudices after experiencing God's leading in this direction. In Galatians 2, however, Peter's old prejudices returned.) **Is it true of you or any of your friends? Explain.**

6. After Cornelius and Peter both shared what God had done for them personally (vss. 27-33)**, what new insight did Peter have** (vss. 34, 35)**?** (God doesn't play favorites, but He accepts all people who fear [respect] Him and do what's right.)

7. As Peter was speaking (vss. 34-43)**, what happened that surprised his Jewish companions** (vss. 44-48)**?** (It became obvious that the Holy Spirit was not limiting His power to Jewish Christians. Though Gentiles had always been excluded as "unclean," God was going to form His church from both groups.)

8. Have you ever been astonished (vs. 45) **or surprised to hear that someone had become a Christian? Who's the last person on earth you'd expect to become one?**

9. As the Jews and Gentiles begin to merge, what good things might you expect to come of it? What problems might you expect?

Use the reproducible sheet, "Do Me a Favor," to further discuss the concept of reaching out to people we might not want to associate with. Cut off the bottom portion and make copies of the top part. Give these out to your group members. Have them select two numbers between 1 and 8. Using the bottom portion of the sheet, tell kids what their numbers represent, and have them fill in the blanks on their sheets accordingly. Then have them answer the questions based on the person and favor they have chosen. Discuss as time allows. **Would any of your answers change if you knew this person was a Christian? Why or why not?**

Do Me A FAVOR

Your youth leader asked you to do a favor for someone and you agreed. The next day you find out what you got yourself into. It seems a person who is

_____ wants you to

(pick a number from 1 to 8 ___)

_____.

(pick a number from 1 to 8 ___)

DON'T EVEN THINK ABOUT TRYING TO GET OUT OF IT.

1. On a scale from 1 (lousy) to 10 (great), how do you feel about doing this favor? _____

2. What might be the hardest thing about following through on this favor?
_____

3. What might be something you'd enjoy about it?
_____

4. What are some prejudices you might have about this person?
_____

5. What are some fears you might have?
_____

6. List three questions you could ask this person to make conversation.
_____

7. List three things you could pray about for this person.
_____

- -

PERSON
1. an inner-city gang member
2. dying of the AIDS virus
3. mentally handicapped
4. an exchange student from Iraq
5. unable to walk or talk
6. a member of a white supremacist group
7. a drug addict
8. very stuck up

FAVOR
1. let him/her stay at your place for a week
2. take him/her to all your classes for a week
3. tutor him/her for three months
4. talk with him/her about your faith
5. go on a double date together
6. share a room together during a church outing
7. take him/her to a school football game
8. take him/her shopping the next three Saturdays

ACTS 11

Critics and Christians

As word spreads that Peter has been spending time with Gentiles and accepting them as fellow believers in Christ, he receives criticism from some of the Jewish believers. But when he gives them more details, they praise God for His acceptance of this other group. The Gospel begins to spread to other Gentile congregations, including one in Antioch, where followers of Jesus are first called "Christians."

Divide your group into guys and girls. Each group will be given a few minutes to do its best imitation of the other (imitating mannerisms, favorite phrases, topics of discussion, etc.). Give groups a few minutes to practice, then have them perform their imitations to each other. If you have a group of all guys or all girls, divide according to some other distinction that lends itself to joking around, like year in school, athlete/non-athlete, organized/unorganized, etc. This activity will probably point out the major differences between the two groups and the stereotypes that each group has of the other. (Yet in spite of all those differences, they've probably discovered that it's kind of fun to hang out together.) And just as the Jews and Gentiles had major differences and strong opinions about each other, they were eventually going to be united under the common bond of Christianity.

DATE I USED THIS SESSION _____ GROUP I USED IT WITH _____

NOTES FOR NEXT TIME _____

_____

_____

1. Who do you think criticizes you the most? Why? Who are you most critical of? Why?

2. As word spread that Peter had spent a couple of days with Gentiles, and that they had been able to believe in Jesus just as the Jews had, some of the Jewish believers started accusing and criticizing Peter (vss. 1-3). **How do you think Peter felt?** (It's bad enough to be criticized anytime. But Peter had just returned from seeing God's love reach out to a whole new group of people. It must have been particularly depressing to come "home" to his Jewish peers, only to hear their immediate criticism.)

3. What can we learn from Peter about handling criticism (vss. 4-17)? (He patiently reviewed the facts for his accusers—the whole story. He also made it clear that his actions had been in obedience to God's instructions, and that the results were thanks to the power of God and nothing he had done on his own.)

4. Why did his critics change their minds (vs. 18)? (They were convinced that this new direction really was of God.)

5. Until this time, the people going throughout the area and spreading the word about Jesus had confined themselves to Jewish groups. But now some of them felt called to speak to the Gentiles as well. Was it worth their efforts (vss. 19-21)? (Yes. In Antioch a "great number" of people believed in Jesus.) **What does this suggest about our own efforts to tell other people about Jesus?** (Perhaps there are people we know who don't seem to have much interest in religious things. But we shouldn't automatically rule them out as being unwilling to listen to us.)

6. During this time, whenever a special need arose in the church, Barnabas could be counted on to help (4:36, 37; 8:26, 27). **So when the word came that Gentiles in Antioch were being converted, that's who they sent. But he didn't stay long at first** (vss. 22-26). **Why not?** (He left to get Saul.) **Why did he do this?** (It seems that Barnabas recognized how much work [and potential] awaited them in Antioch. Barnabas seemed to recognize how much potential the new convert, Saul, had.) **If you could choose someone to be your partner for some type of ministry, who would you choose and why?**

7. **Antioch was the first place that followers of Jesus were called Christians (vs. 26). The name means "belonging to Christ." What do you think the name "Christian" means to most people today?** (Some might suggest that recent scandals involving televangelists and other religious leaders have given Christians a bad name. Others might associate the name "Christian" with people who live by Christian values, but who haven't necessarily made a personal commitment to follow Christ.)

8. **We see another example of early believers pitching in to help each other out in verses 27 through 30. Give some examples of similar types of "help" that we can offer today.** (Relief efforts for third world countries; support of missionaries; local food pantries, etc.)

The reproducible sheet, "Name Game," will challenge students to create new words based on the names of the people in the group (much like "Christians" was invented to mean "associated with Christ.") When they finish, let them share their new words. Then discuss: **In wearing the name "Christian," do you ever feel a sense of pride? Embarrassment? Fear? What else do you feel? Why do you feel each of these things?**

NAME G·A·M·E

NICE RUDOLPHBERRY, MR. BOYSEN!

Christianity is named after a person—Jesus Christ. At the bottom of this sheet, you'll get a chance to coin some new words or phrases to honor the names of people in your group. But first, here's a little practice. Can you figure out what has been named after each of the following people?

1. Adolphe Sax
(Belgian musical instrument maker)

_____

2. Mr. and Mrs. Legrand Benedict
(People who liked to cook)

_____

3. Rudolph Boysen (Horticulturist)

_____

4. John Macadam (Australian chemist)

_____

5. Josh Billings (19th Century humorist)

_____

6. Joel Roberts Pointsett
(U.S. Ambassador to Mexico)

_____

7. Frederick S. Duesenburg
(Automobile manufacturer)

_____

8. Alessandro Volta (Italian physicist)

_____

9. Franz Anton Mesmer (Austrian physician)

_____

10. Arnold Reuben (New York deli owner)

_____

Now, here's your chance. Come up with a new phrase that pays tribute to the following people. Be sure to define your phrase. For example, if someone in your group is named Rick, and he's good in sports, then your word for a great athlete might be a "rickman." If Mindy likes to cook, a new word for good cooking might be "mindylicious."

Your youth leader/teacher:_____

Yourself:_____

Others in your group:_____

Answers - (1) Saxophone; (2) Eggs Benedict; (3) Boysenberry; (4) Macadamia nut; (5) The phrase, "joshing around"; (6) Poinsettia; (7) The phrase, "a real doozey"; (8) The volt; (9) The word, "mesmerized"; (10) The reuben sandwich.

ACTS 12

Jailbreak!

The persecution of the church intensifies as one of Jesus' original disciples—James—is put to death by Herod. Then Peter is arrested, but an angel helps him escape. Soon afterward, Herod takes credit for acclaim he doesn't deserve, and dies.

(Needed: Three hymnals)

Hand out the top portion of the reproducible sheet, "Truth or Dare." Have kids answer the questions without looking in their Bibles. Tell them that these questions all come from the passage you'll study today. Call on a "volunteer" to answer question one. The volunteer can stay seated if he/she gets it right. (Answers: [1] a; [2] c; [3] c; [4] c; [5] d; [6] c; [7] a; [8] b; [9] b; [10] d.) If wrong, however, he/she must do one of the dares that you choose. These are listed on the bottom of the sheet. If the dares listed don't seem appropriate, come up with your own. Explain that anyone can appeal to the group to be excused; group members respond with thumbs up (to let the person off) or thumbs down (to make him or her go through with it). Majority wins. More than likely, not many people will be excused. Continue with the other questions following the same procedure. Use this to show that some people seem to enjoy seeing others suffer.

DATE I USED THIS SESSION _____ GROUP I USED IT WITH _____

NOTES FOR NEXT TIME _____

_____

_____

1. Have you ever been glad to see someone else suffer or mess up on something? Or have you ever joined in with a group of people giving someone a hard time? If so, describe the situation. Why do people sometimes enjoy seeing others suffer?

2. Unfortunately, some people seem to thrive on the sufferings of others. In this case, King Herod had put James, one of Jesus' original disciples, to death. The Jewish leaders were so happy about it that Herod went out and arrested Peter right away (vss. 1-4). Be honest . . . if the government suddenly began hauling in Christians for arrest or even death, what do you think you would do? **What did the first-century church do** (vs. 5)? (Though they were meeting behind locked doors [vs. 13], they were gathered together, praying about the situation.)

3. This appeared to be a maximum security prison. Read verse 6. If you were Peter, and got to make one phone call from jail, who would you call, and what would you say? **How worried was Peter?** (Even though security was tight and things probably looked pretty grim, Peter doesn't appear to have been too worried, considering the fact that he was sleeping.)

4. What woke him up (vs. 7)? (He was struck in the side.) What would be the first thing to go through your mind if this happened?

5. Peter didn't really believe what happened next (vss. 7-10). **Why not?** (Peter had received visions from God previously [10:9-16]. Perhaps he thought this was just a nice dream.)

6. When did Peter finally realize that he had actually been rescued (vs. 11)? (After the angel left and he was standing, free, on the street a block from the prison.)

7. Keep in mind that the church members have been holed up, praying for Peter (vss. 5, 12). **What do you think of their response when he showed up unexpectedly** (vss. 12-15)? (The one person who heard him was so excited that she forgot to open the door. But the others refused to believe that he was truly there.) **Why do you think they didn't believe, since that's exactly what they were praying about?** (Perhaps they didn't believe Peter would [or could] be delivered prior to his trial. Maybe they were praying for Peter, but not necessarily for his release.)

8. Do you ever pray for things you don't actually believe will happen? If so, give some examples.

9. What result did Peter's escape have on the church (vss. 16, 17)? (Astonishment at God's power.) **On the guards (vss. 18, 19)?** (Execution.)

10. But Herod, the leader whose pride had caused so much trouble for so many people, was about to go too far. People had learned to flatter Herod to get what they wanted, but what happened in this instance (vss. 19-23)? (He was praised for being a god, and didn't dispute it. Consequently, the true God struck him down on the spot and Herod died a humiliating death.)

11. After all the events in this chapter, the Word of God continued to spread (vss. 24, 25). **What effect do hard times have on you?**

Challenge group members to avoid making the same mistake Herod made of assuming he alone was responsible for the position and power he had been given. Encourage kids to mention things they've been given (talents, possessions, accomplishments, etc.), and then spend some time in prayer, giving God the credit for these things.

TRUTH OR *DARE*

1. Who was king at the time the chapter opens?
   - a. Herod
   - b. Agrippa
   - c. Claudius
   - d. Festus

2. Who was the first of the original disciples to be martyred?
   - a. Judas
   - b. Peter
   - c. James
   - d. John

3. During what Jewish holiday was Peter thrown in jail?
   - a. Pentecost, the Feast of Weeks
   - b. Tabernacles, the Feast of Booths
   - c. Passover, the Feast of Unleavened Bread
   - d. Hanukkah, the Feast of Dedication

4. How many soldiers guarded Peter?
   - a. none
   - b. 6
   - c. 16
   - d. 26

5. How did the angel wake Peter up?
   - a. a bright light
   - b. a loud noise
   - c. an earthquake
   - d. he hit him

6. Who answered the door when Peter arrived at the house where people were praying?
   - a. Mary
   - b. Phyllis
   - c. Rhoda
   - d. No one—the people inside were too afraid

7. Who was a trusted personal servant of King Herod?
   - a. Blastus
   - b. Bacchus
   - c. Barsabbas
   - d. Barak

8. Why did Herod die?
   - a. He cursed God
   - b. He didn't praise God
   - c. He didn't make sacrifices to God
   - d. He withheld money from God

9. How did Herod die?
   - a. Knifed in the back by his own guard
   - b. Eaten by worms
   - c. In his sleep
   - d. Bow and arrow

10. Who did Barnabas and Saul take with them when they left Jerusalem?
    - a. Peter
    - b. Timothy
    - c. Luke
    - d. Mark

D A R E S

1. Do 20 push-ups.

2. Sing "Twinkle, Twinkle Little Star" as loud as you can.

3. Hold a hymnal in each hand with arms outstretched for two minutes while balancing a third hymnal on your head. (Continue with the other questions in the meantime.)

4. Imitate a pig for 30 seconds.

5. Balance on one foot with eyes closed for one minute.

6. Tell about your first kiss (or get down on one knee and kiss the hand of someone else in the group).

7. Tie everyone's untied shoes.

8. Impersonate a famous person until someone guesses who it is.

9. Whistle a television theme song until people guess it—no laughing.

10. Draw your self portrait—using your feet only!

ACTS 13

Bon Voyage

The Holy Spirit calls Barnabas and Saul from the church in Antioch to work together to carry the Gospel message to other areas. So they begin their first missionary journey. It is during this journey that the writer of Acts begins referring to Saul as "Paul." Paul and Barnabas are received with mixed reactions as they are frequently opposed by the Jewish leaders and welcomed by the Gentiles.

Have your group form a circle. Select one player to begin. He or she should name any town or city. The person on the right must then name another town or city that begins with the last letter of the one just mentioned. The next player should do the same, and so on. Give each person just five seconds to come up with a name. If someone can't come up with one, he or she is out. Here's an example chain: London-New York-Knoxville-Edmonton-Niagara Falls-Sarasota. No player can use a city or town already mentioned. When the chain is broken, the next person in line should start a new chain. If your group is large, consider playing this game in several circles, and have the winners of the different circles play against each other. In this chapter, Paul begins his extensive travels. Taking the Gospel to other places becomes a lifelong mission for him.

DATE I USED THIS SESSION _____ GROUP I USED IT WITH _____

NOTES FOR NEXT TIME _____

_____

_____

1. What's the most exciting trip or vacation you've ever been on?

2. In this chapter, Saul and Barnabas begin a two-man missions trip. What motivated them to go (vss. 1-3)? (They had been working together for a while in Antioch [11:25, 26]. But this trip was in response to a call of the Holy Spirit.)

3. One of the first stops for Saul and Barnabas was the island of Cyprus, where good news awaited. A local official sent for them because he wanted to hear the Word of God. But what threatened to keep them from teaching Paulus (vss. 4-8)? (Paulus had another advisor—a sorcerer and false prophet. If Paulus believed Saul and Barnabas, then the sorcerer would lose the position of authority he had established.)

4. Can you think of ways that Christianity seems threatening to some people, even today? (Yielding to the will of God; tough teachings like the existence of hell, etc.)

5. How did Saul deal with this particular threat (vss. 9-11)? (With the power of God, he inflicted the sorcerer with temporary blindness.) What was the result (vs. 12)? (The miracle convinced Sergius Paulus of the power of God, and consequently, the truth of the Gospel. He became a believer as a result.)

6. Why do you suppose Saul's name changed to Paul (vs. 9)? (Saul is a Hebrew name; Paul is more of a Roman name. This reflects his new emphasis to take the Gospel to Gentile regions.)

7. Paul and Barnabas had picked up Barnabas's cousin, John Mark, along the way (vs. 5). But at this point, for an unexplained reason, John Mark leaves them. This parting will later cause conflict between Paul and Barnabas (15:36-41). Have you ever made a commitment to do something, but changed your mind after you got into it? (This is a common occurrence for young people as they try out a lot of things in order to see what they enjoy and are good at. But point out the importance of sticking with Christian commitment—even if it seems a little burdensome from time to time.)

8. **In the next town Paul again presented the Gospel very clearly** (vss. 13-41). **What is some of the "good news" that Paul included in his talk?** (God has sent a message of salvation through Jesus. This message is for both Jews and Gentiles. God fulfilled His promise by sending His Son and raising Him from the dead. Through Him, we can receive forgiveness for sins.) **In what ways were people's reactions to Paul's message similar to the ways people respond to the Good News today** (vss. 42-52)? (Some believed; some had their curiosity aroused and wanted to hear more; some were openly hostile.)

9. **What can we learn from how Paul and Barnabas responded to those who didn't want to believe?** (When we share about Jesus, not everyone will accept the message. When this happens, we shouldn't take it personally; rather, we should seek out others who might be more open.)

Paul and Barnabas were excellent missionaries. They were aware of the need to tell people in other places about Jesus, and they were sent to share this good news. Use the reproducible sheet, "The World outside Your Door," to get your kids thinking about some of the needs in the world. All true/false answers are "true," and all multiple choice answers are "d." Discuss: **Which of these questions surprise you? What are some of the needs identified here?** (Food; clean water; to hear the Gospel; Bible translation; illiteracy; poverty; more people living in cities, which will cause more pollution, etc.) **What can we possibly do to make a difference in a world with so many needs?**

THE WORLD OUTSIDE YOUR DOOR

The world is a pretty needy place. Just how needy is it? Answer these questions to find out:

TRUE/FALSE

1. _____ Over 500 million people in the world are severely malnourished.

2. _____ There's enough food in the world to adequately feed every person twice over.

3. _____ More people in the world claim to be Christian than any other religion.

4. _____ The whole Bible has been translated into about 5% of the known languages of the world.

5. _____ Over half of the 250,000 children under 5 who die each week could live if they had adequate food and access to medical attention.

6. _____ Over 80% of Muslims have never heard the Gospel.

MULTIPLE CHOICE

1. In industrial countries, about 95% of those employed receive regular wages. What's the percentage who receive regular wages in developing countries?
    a. 90%   c. 25%   b. 50%   d. 10%

2. How many distinct cultural groups in the world don't have a Christian witness in them?
    a. 16   c. 1,600   b. 160   d. 16,000

3. In North America, the average life expectancy of males is a little over 72 years. What is it for males in Afghanistan?
    a. 77   c. 57   b. 67   d. 37

4. What percent of the world's population lives in shelter considered less than adequate by the United Nations?
    a. 5%   c. 15%   b. 10%   d. 25%

5. What percent of the world's water supply is fresh water?
    a. 94%   c. 24%   b. 51%   d. 2.4%

6. How many people in the world die each day as a result of drinking unsafe water?
    a. 25   c. 2,500   b. 250   d. 25,000

7. What percentage of all deaths in the world are of children under 5 years old?
    a. 3%   c. 23%   b. 13%   d. 33%

8. What percent of African adults are illiterate (can't read)?
    a. 10%   c. 45%   b. 25%   d. 70%

9. What percent of the world's population doesn't have radio or television?
    a. 7%   c. 47%   b. 17%   d. 67%

10. The world's rural population has doubled since 1950. How about urban population?
    a. -10%   c. +100%   b. +10%   d. +1000%

ACTS 14

Paul's Close Call

Paul and Barnabas continue to meet with mixed reactions as they spread the Gospel. As people see God's power demonstrated, some attribute it to His human messengers and assume Paul and Barnabas are Greek gods. With difficulty, the two convince the crowd otherwise, after which the people go to the other extreme and stone Paul, leaving him for dead. But he and Barnabas simply move on to encourage people in other places.

(Needed: Decks of cards; old newspapers)

Divide into teams of about three or four, and give each team a deck of cards and a supply of newspaper. Set a time limit and see which team can build the largest "house of cards." The only catch is that some team members should throw newspaper wads at the other teams' houses while they're trying to build, attempting to knock the houses down. Set boundaries so that kids have to throw from a distance. At the end of the time limit, see which team has been able to build the most elaborate house.

DATE I USED THIS SESSION _____ GROUP I USED IT WITH _____

NOTES FOR NEXT TIME _____

_____

_____

1. Have you ever worked very hard to succeed at something, only to have someone ruin your efforts (or try to)? Explain.

2. As Paul and Barnabas continued to travel around and talk about Jesus, there were a lot of people who believed. But what kept the two from getting a better response (vss. 1, 2)? (Paul and Barnabas would traditionally speak at the local Jewish synagogues, and many of the Jewish leaders took offense to their message. These opponents would do everything in their power to prevent others from believing the truth about Jesus.)

3. How bad did the opposition get (vss. 3-5)? (A plot was under way to have Paul and Barnabas stoned.) **If you were the target of such a plan, what do you think you would do?** (Lie low for a while, "soften" your message a bit, go home and keep your mouth shut, etc.) **What did Paul and Barnabas do** (vss. 6, 7)? (They wisely moved on to the next town, but kept boldly proclaiming the same message.)

4. In addition to preaching sermons, how did Paul and Barnabas show that they represented a loving, caring God (vss. 8-10)? (They also had the power to perform miracles. In this case, Paul healed a man who had been lame since birth.)

5. The crowd's reaction to this miracle was completely unexpected (vss. 11-13). **What happened?** (The people mistook Paul and Barnabas for Hermes and Zeus—two of the main Greek gods.)

6. How did Paul and Barnabas respond (vss. 14-18)? (They immediately tried to refute the claims with both their words and actions, though they weren't very successful.)

7. Imagine you're part of the crowd (vs. 19). **What things do you hear the Jewish leaders from Antioch saying to "win the crowd over"?** (Perhaps the Jewish leaders tried to make Paul and Barnabas' claims sound silly, or maybe they pointed out ways that Paul and Barnabas were just ordinary men.)

8. Have you ever had people saying bad things about you? If so, how did this make you feel?

9. What was Paul's attitude after being stoned and left for dead (vss. 20-22)? (Amazingly enough, Paul continued to travel and encourage other people. He didn't expect a "pity party" from anyone, and wrote off this experience as one of the "many hardships" he would experience before entering the kingdom of God.)

10. Since Paul and Barnabas were on the road so often, how did they see to the continued growth of the churches they visited (vs. 23)? (They appointed elders in each church to carry on the work.) **If Paul and Barnabas visited your church, who do you think they'd appoint as "elders"?**

11. What specific things do you suppose Paul and Barnabas reported to the church in Antioch (vss. 24-28)? (Review events from chapters 13 and 14.)

In Acts 14:22, Paul and Barnabas said, "We must go through many hardships to enter the kingdom of God." While this can't be taken as a requirement for their salvation, it certainly was a result of it. The reproducible sheet, "It's a Hard Life," will help your kids think about some of the hardships Christians might face today. After giving them a few minutes to read the situations, share your lists together. Then talk about any hardships your group members might be facing.

IT'S A HARD LIFE

If you're living your life for Jesus, you can expect your share of hard times. Read the following cases and list some of the hardships these people might face as a result of their faith.

Lee wants to know more about the Bible. He has an idea to start an early morning Bible study at school before classes meet.
People who might give him a hard time:

Some of the hardships he might face:

Keesha is convinced that abortion is wrong and wants to do something about it. She joined a pro-life group. Tomorrow she's planning to picket a local clinic.
People who might give her a hard time:

Some of the hardships she might face:

Carlos has been very attracted to the gay lifestyle. Some of his best friends are gay. He just became a Christian and feels he needs to make a clean break from this group of friends.
People who might give him a hard time:

Some of the hardships he might face:

Cindy is on the student council. Others on the council want to organize a drive to distribute free condoms to all the students to fight the spread of AIDS. Cindy feels that this approach is wrong because it could encourage premarital sex.
People who might give her a hard time:

Some of the hardships she might face:

Wise Council

Some of the Jewish believers in Antioch are trying to make circumcision a requirement for belief in Jesus. Paul and Barnabas travel to Jerusalem to discuss the matter with the apostles and elders. After hearing from Peter, Paul, and Barnabas, the council decides that Gentile circumcision isn't necessary. Later, as Paul and Barnabas prepare to return to the churches they had previously visited, a conflict over John Mark causes them to go their separate ways.

(Needed: Slips of paper with words for kids to draw)

Prepare a list of words that might suggest certain stereotypes to your young people (girl, jock, movie star, model, freak, honor student, etc.). Put these words on separate slips of paper. Hand someone a slip and have the person draw the image as the other group members try to guess what it is. To make it more of a challenge, explain that no symbols, letters, or numbers can be used as clues. Then give the next person a slip, and so on. To add excitement, divide into two teams and have a representative from each team draw the same word and see which team guesses it first. The last word should be "Christian." See what stereotypes are used to convey the image (since a cross symbol can't be drawn). From this, discuss the expected "image" of a Christian, and work your way into the session.

DATE I USED THIS SESSION _____ GROUP I USED IT WITH _____

NOTES FOR NEXT TIME_____

_____

_____

1. What's the most uncomfortable outfit you've ever worn?

2. As the early church began to expand to include Gentiles, a lot of the Jewish believers became uncomfortable. To them, a man was only acceptable to God if he had been circumcised. Some were teaching this as truth (vs. 1). What's the first thing Paul and Barnabas did to argue against such teaching (vss. 2-4)? (They had just returned from visiting several cities where they had seen many Gentiles believe in Jesus and receive the Holy Spirit, just as the Jewish believers in Antioch and Jerusalem had done.)

3. Where was much of the Jewish legalism coming from (vs. 5)? Why? (Some of the Pharisees, who had been defending Mosaic law for so long, were becoming Christians. They felt a man should convert to Judaism first, including being circumcised, and then go from there to becoming a Christian.)

4. What are some of the issues that divide Christians in similar ways today? (Hair length; church dress expectations; expression of spiritual gifts, etc.)

5. What arguments did the "no need for circumcision" people use (vss. 6-18)? (Peter testified that God had sent him to start the whole Gospel-to-the-Gentiles movement [Acts 10]; Paul and Barnabas further detailed the miracles they had seen God perform among the Gentiles; and James quoted Old Testament Scripture to show God's intent to one day include the Gentile peoples in His kingdom.)

6. The final verdict was that the Gentiles need not be circumcised to become believers. But there were some other matters the council felt were important. What common Gentile practices were of concern to the early Christians (vss. 19-21)? (Eating foods associated with the worship of idols; eating meat from which the blood had not yet been removed, or partaking of blood separately; and sexual immorality.)

7. The decision of the council was taken back to the church in Antioch by letter (vss. 22-29). This was a major

point of conflict that might have split the church at a very early (and vulnerable) time. What was the result (vss. 30-35)? (The people were glad and encouraged [though the circumcision debate would come up again later].)

8. Meanwhile, another conflict was splitting up Paul and Barnabas. What was it (vss. 36-38)? (Barnabas wanted to try once more to take his cousin, John Mark, with them on this next journey. The first time they had taken him, he had deserted them [Acts 13:5, 13]. Barnabas wanted to give Mark another chance. Paul didn't.)

9. Who do you think was right—Paul or Barnabas? (Arguments can be made both ways. This work was too important to have someone who wasn't totally committed. Yet we all occasionally need forgiveness and second chances.)

10. How was the conflict resolved (vss. 39-41)? (Barnabas partnered with John Mark, and Paul set out with another disciple named Silas.)

Make two lists on the board—positive and negative ways to deal with conflict. Then read through the roleplays on the reproducible sheet, "Take Two." Assign parts for each role-play. First, your characters should act out a negative way to deal with the conflict, then they should deal with it positively. If your kids are uncomfortable acting, you could simply discuss positive and negative ways to deal with these situations. After going through the roleplays, discuss conflict situations your kids are facing, and some constructive ways to deal with them.

It's the chance of a lifetime—an acting audition. Here are the situations to act out. In the first take, deal with the conflict situation in a negative way. In the second take, do it right.

SCENE 1 - Your youth group is going on a ski trip. In order to keep the number of people to a decent level, your leader says that only members of the group are allowed to go. You're disappointed because one of your friends really loves to ski. On the day of the trip, you find out that several people are bringing friends from outside the group anyway. You're miffed at your leader.

Roles: You and your youth leader. Setting: Riding in the car on the way to the ski lodge.

Your opening line (negative):_____

Your opening line (positive): _____

SCENE 2 - You get in a minor car accident in your family car (you're sure it was the other person's fault even though he wasn't ticketed). Now you have to break the news to your parents. By the way, the car was brand new and you hadn't asked to borrow it.

Roles: You and your mom and/or dad. Setting: At home, watching TV.

Your opening line (negative): _____

Your opening line (positive): _____

SCENE 3 - One of your friends from church has started hanging around with a new group of people, and you've been noticing that your friend is suddenly a lot less friendly. One day at school your friend totally ignores you. You feel hurt.

Roles: You and your friend. Setting: A week later, at church.

Your opening line (negative): _____

Your opening line (positive): _____

ACTS 16

The Jailhouse Rocks

Paul sets off on his second missionary journey, this time with Silas, and soon they add young Timothy to their team. God provides clear direction where they are to go, and the response to the Gospel is good. However, opponents have them thrown into jail, where they sing and praise God. An earthquake rocks the prison, and Paul shows the jailer that salvation is a far better solution than suicide.

(Needed: One coin for each person)

Give each person in your group, including yourself, a coin. As you flip your coin, everyone else should do likewise. Those that match you get to stay in, those that don't are out. Keep playing until everyone is eliminated. Let the last person (or people) to be eliminated keep the coin(s). Play other rounds if there's time. Use this activity to talk about ways we sometimes make decisions. With the Holy Spirit to guide us, we certainly don't need to flip coins—something Paul and Silas experience in this chapter.

DATE I USED THIS SESSION _____ GROUP I USED IT WITH _____

NOTES FOR NEXT TIME _____

_____

_____

1. Have you ever struggled with an important decision, wondering what God's will was for you? If so, share how you decided what to do.

2. Why did Paul and Silas decide to have Timothy join their team (vss. 1-5)? (He had developed a reputation for good character among the local church leaders. Perhaps Timothy had become a Christian during Paul's previous visit, and Paul wanted to help him develop his faith. Maybe Paul wanted someone from that immediate area as another witness to God's power to change lives. Or perhaps Paul wanted Timothy to take over the things John Mark had done on the first trip [13:5].)

3. The church leaders had just ruled that circumcision was not a necessary step for becoming a Christian (Acts 15). So why do you think Paul wanted Timothy to be circumcised (vss. 3-5)? (It had nothing to do with salvation. Many of Paul's hearers would be Jewish, and having an uncircumcised man whose mother was Jewish [vs. 1] might have unnecessarily impaired the effectiveness of Paul's teaching.)

4. What do verses 6 through 10 tell us about finding God's will for our lives? (Sometimes God closes doors for us—His Spirit might prevent us from doing things, even things that may seem right at the time. Though Paul's intention was to follow up in many of the places that he had visited previously [15:36], God had other plans for Paul and Silas.) How might they have been prevented from doing what they planned to do? When your plans change unexpectedly, how do you usually feel about it?

5. Notice in verse 10 that the person telling the story shifts from using words like "they" to "we." What do you suppose is the reason for this? (Luke, the writer of Acts, appears to join the travelers in Troas.)

6. What happened when the group got to Philippi (vss. 11-15)? (The people seemed to be very responsive. One in particular, named Lydia, immediately gave the disciples her support.)

7. But then what happened that caused Paul and Silas some trouble (vss. 16-24)? (Paul removed an evil spirit from a girl, eliminating her ability to make money for her masters. Paul and Silas were beaten and thrown into prison.)

8. Far away from home and in prison, how would you feel? How did Paul and Silas act (vs. 25)? And because their emphasis was on praising God rather than getting out of jail, what was the result (vss. 26-34)? (When an earthquake set the prisoners free, Paul and Silas turned the occasion into a revival meeting rather than an escape party. The jailer, who assumed the Roman authorities would hold him accountable for escaped prisoners, was stopped from committing suicide and found a secure future in Jesus instead.) Why might some people today feel that suicide is their only option? What would you say to someone who was contemplating suicide?

9. If you had to write a song about the events in verses 25 through 34, what would the title of your song be?

10. Word was sent the next morning that Paul and Silas could be released. But why didn't they go right away (vss. 35-40)? (As Roman citizens, they had rights that had been violated. They should not have been beaten—much less without a trial.) Why do you think Paul demanded that the magistrates come to the prison and release them personally? (Perhaps he wanted them to think twice before doing the same thing to the next people who came along. And he probably wanted a public acknowledgment of the innocence of his party so his work would not be hindered.)

(Needed: Songbooks; guitar or piano [optional])

Hand out copies of the hymnbook and/or songbook that your church uses in worship, along with the student sheet, "Can You Hum a Few Bars?" Have kids search through the hymnals/songbooks for songs that would be appropriate to sing or think about during each of the crises listed. Choose several songs to sing or read together.

CAN YOU HUM A FEW BARS?

uppose you're in a new town, minding your own business, when suddenly you're arrested and thrown in jail. What do you do? You sing, right? Probably not—but that's exactly what Paul and Silas did. Choose a hymn or other Christian song that would be good to sing (or think about) in each of the following situations.

1. You're taking a test. Suddenly you freeze up and can't remember any of the answers.

_____

_____

2. Last Friday night you got home about an hour after you were supposed to. Your parents didn't buy your excuse that your watch stopped, so they grounded you for two weeks. Now it's the next Friday, and you feel like a prisoner in your own home.

_____

_____

3. You return from your favorite Mexican restaurant, Los Puercos, stuffed to the gills from their Tuesday night "All the Meat You Can Eat" buffet. About an hour later, you discover—the hard way—that some of their guacamole must have sat out a little too long. Unfortunately, you are reminded of that fact many times during the night.

_____

_____

4. Your parents are away for a couple of weeks as you go through a massive breakup with your boyfriend/girlfriend. You've never felt more alone.

_____

_____

5. A very close friend has been in a severe car accident. You're waiting for news in the hospital waiting room.

_____

_____

ACTS 17

It's Greek to Me

The missionary journey of Paul and Silas takes them to Thessalonica, Berea, and Athens. In some cases, they are persecuted, as are the people who try to help them. In other cases, their hearers diligently check out the things they are teaching. And in Athens, Paul finds a creative way to overcome initial resistance to the Gospel.

(Needed: Calculators, NIV Bibles, small prize [optional])

Form teams for this Scripture-searching activity. Give each team a calculator, a New International Version (NIV) Bible, and a copy of the reproducible sheet, "Crunching Numbers." See which team can arrive at the correct final total most quickly. The correct answer is zero. (Solution: 150 times 31, plus 27,000, divided by 3, plus 700, plus 10, minus 1,260, minus 10,000, plus 666, minus 666, plus 7, minus 7, equals 0.) Give a prize to the winning team if you wish. In this chapter your group will learn about the Bereans, who also were known for searching the Scripture. **In the game we just played, we ended up with nothing, but if we eagerly examine the Scriptures on a regular basis, like the Bereans did, we'll certainly get something out of it!**

DATE I USED THIS SESSION _____ GROUP I USED IT WITH _____

NOTES FOR NEXT TIME _____

_____

_____

1. Can you think of a time when you've been really jealous of someone? What were you jealous of? Has anyone ever been jealous of you? How did this person show his or her jealousy?

2. Why were the Jewish leaders jealous of Paul and his companions (vss. 1-5)? (Because some of the Jewish people were threatened by the things Paul and Silas were saying. The religious leaders probably weren't getting the same kind of response from people, especially the prominent ones.)

3. How did they deal with their jealousy (vs. 5-9)? (They started a riot, hoping to hurt Paul and the others.) **How do you deal with your jealousy?**

4. Contrast the people in Berea with those in Thessalonica (vss. 10-12). What lesson can we learn from them? (The Bereans were eager to respond, though they wanted to make sure Scripture backed up what Paul and Silas were saying. We should also study Scripture to find out what it really says.)

5. So why didn't the Berean ministry flourish (vs. 13)? (Because the troublemakers from Thessalonica had followed Paul and Silas and continued to try to stir up the crowds against them.)

6. How did Paul and crew combat this kind of persecution (vss. 14, 15)? (They split up. Paul, the most vocal and visible of the group, moved on to Athens. Silas and Timothy stayed behind to follow up in Berea. Persecution simply doubled the spreading of the Gospel.)

7. What were the pros and cons Paul found in Athens (vss. 16-21)? (The abundance of idols was depressing. But on the other hand, it allowed him to speak freely about Jesus, the Son of the one true God. The people were open-minded.)

8. What was the first result of Paul's introducing the truth about God to a group of people who tended to worship many gods? (At first they were confused and accused him of "babbling," but their curiosity was aroused to the point that they wanted to hear more.)

9. **How did Paul get the attention of these curious, but skeptical, Greeks** (vss. 22-31)**?** (He found one of their altars offering praise "To an unknown god." With the many gods and goddesses the Greeks tried to appease, this was no doubt a "catchall" altar in case they missed one. But Paul used this to suggest, "No, you don't know this God, but I do. And let me tell you about Him." Paul also had a knowledge of Greek literature, and quoted some of their own poets to make his point in a place or two.)

10. **How did the Greek listeners respond to Paul's description of a single, living God with power to raise people from the dead, as opposed to the multitude of man-made gods that were represented in this area** (vss. 32-34)**?** (Like most other places, he had his share of scoffers. But others followed him and eventually believed in Jesus.)

Contrast the different reactions the three towns in this chapter (Thessalonica, Berea, and Athens) had to the Gospel. Ask: **Which of these three towns would you fit into best? Why?** Then discuss the importance of regular Bible study, following the example of the Bereans. Choose a passage of Scripture (perhaps Acts 18) to study this week, and challenge kids to spend a few minutes in Bible study every day this week.

CRUNCHING NUMBERS

Look up the following numbers in the Bible, perform the mathematical calculations, and see who can arrive at the final total first.

Number of chapters in the Book of Psalms
Times the number of chapters in the Book of Proverbs   x _____

    = _____

Plus the number of men killed in I Kings 20:30   + _____

    = _____

Divided by the number of decks on Noah's ark (Genesis 6:16)   ÷ _____

    = _____

Plus the number of wives Solomon had—not
counting concubines (I Kings 11:3)   + _____

    = _____

Plus the number of lepers in Luke 17:12   + _____

    = _____

Minus the number of days in Revelation 12:6   - _____

    = _____

Minus the number of rivers of oil in Micah 6:7   - _____

    = _____

Plus the number of descendants of Adonikam (Ezra 2:13)   + _____

    = _____

Minus the weight of gold (in talents) Solomon
received yearly (I Kings 10:14)   - _____

    = _____

Plus the number of sneezes in II Kings 4:32-36   + _____

    = _____

Minus the number of times marched around the city
(Joshua 6:15)   - _____

EQUALS THE FINAL TOTAL   = _____

ACTS 18

The Traveling Tentmaker

Paul travels to Corinth where he makes some new friends and spends time making tents with them. He reasons with the Jews and Greeks in the synagogue and reunites with Silas and Timothy. Paul is again taken to court, but is soon released. He continues his journey as Apollos begins a public ministry as well.

Cut apart the squares on the reproducible sheet, "What's My Line?" Form two teams. Divide the cards in half. Select one person from each team to come forward. The object of this game is to have team members guess the occupation written at the top of each card. But the person giving the clues can't say any of the words listed under the occupation. Have the person from Team 1 go first. Give him or her one minute to give clues. When an occupation is guessed, or when a forbidden word is spoken, go on to the next card. Each card must be played until it is guessed, or time runs out. You should look over the clue-giver's shoulder to make sure none of the forbidden words (or any form of the forbidden words) is spoken. Give the team one point for every occupation guessed correctly. Give the other team one point for any forbidden words that are spoken. In this chapter we see that, in addition to being a missionary, Paul was a tentmaker.

DATE I USED THIS SESSION _____ GROUP I USED IT WITH _____

NOTES FOR NEXT TIME _____

_____

_____

1. What you would consider to be the ideal job?

2. Why do you think Paul spent some time as a tent-maker in addition to all the preaching he did (vss. 1-4)? (He didn't want to be a financial burden on others. See Acts 20:34; I Thessalonians 2:9; II Thessalonians 3:8. He didn't want to be accused of "being in it for the money," either. He also might have enjoyed working with his hands and working together with his friends. This shows we can serve God in many types of work.)

3. When Silas and Timothy rejoined Paul (see 17:14), he returned to full-time preaching and teaching. He was again opposed by many of the Jews in the synagogue. Paul himself was from a highly educated Jewish background. How do you think he felt when his fellow Hebrews wouldn't listen to him (vss. 5, 6)? (He grew very frustrated and followed his usual pattern of then turning to the Gentiles in the area.) How far did he have to travel to find some ready listeners (vss. 7, 8)? (Next door.)

4. Can you think of anyone "next door" (in your immediate neighborhood) who may not have heard the good news about Jesus? How about "next door" to your locker at school? How about "next door" to other places you go on a regular basis?

5. Paul's job must have been a lonely one—always standing in opposition to the crowd and moving from town to town. What happened in Corinth to change that, at least for a while (vss. 9-11)? (God let him know how much he was needed there, and Paul ended up staying for a year and a half.)

6. But eventually, the same thing happened that happened elsewhere—Paul's opponents made trouble for him. This time they took him to court (vss. 12, 13). Paul didn't even get to give his defense this time. Why not (vss. 14-17)? (Before he had the opportunity, the proconsul threw the case out of court.)

7. When Paul was freed, who "took the rap" instead? (Sosthenes, the synagogue ruler, was beaten. Perhaps he had replaced Crispus, the synagogue leader whom Paul had just led to Christianity [vs. 8]. And, unable to bring a case against Paul, he received the effects of the dissatisfaction of his peers.)

8. From Corinth, Paul went on his way, passing through Ephesus and other cities (vss. 18-23). How would you describe Paul's attitude about the future, based on verse 21? (He realized that all his plans were subject to God's will.)

9. Meanwhile, another teacher came to Ephesus. What kind of person was this man, Apollos (vss. 24-28)? What were his strengths and weaknesses? (He seemed very much like Paul in training, knowledge of Scripture, and bold speaking style. His beliefs needed a little shaping, but Priscilla and Aquila helped take care of that.)

10. Who are the Priscillas and Aquilas in your life—people who help explain things about God to you (vs. 26)?

This chapter ends with Apollos "proving from the Scriptures that Jesus was the Christ." Divide into groups of three, and have each group develop a strategy for "proving" from the Bible that Jesus was the Messiah—perhaps to a Jewish person who is familiar with the Old Testament. Obviously, not everyone will believe, but only those who accept Jesus on faith. However, we can still build some pretty convincing arguments. If kids don't know where to begin looking in the Old Testament, direct them to Isaiah 53. After a few minutes, share your strategies.

WHAT'S MY LINE?

Doctor	**Missionary**	**Chef**	**Concert Pianist**
• Medical • Nurse • Hospital • Ph. D. • Surgeon	• Christian • Overseas • Jesus • Church • Foreign	• Food • Restaurant • Baker • Cook • Kitchen	• Piano • Music • Symphony • Play • Notes
Florist	**Accountant**	**Teacher**	**Judge**
• Flowers • Plants • Arrange • Wedding • Bouquet	• Numbers • Tax • Calculator • CPA • Audit	• School • Class • Apple • Learn • Grade	• Law • Court • Jury • Gavel • Trial
Farmer	**Editor**	**Police Officer**	**Homemaker**
• Crops • Grow • Tractor • Rural • Harvest	• Newspaper • Clark Kent • Words • Copy • Proofread	• Cop • Law • Squad car • Arrest • Gun	• Housewife • Children • Mother • Stay • Work
Barber	**Pilot**	**Lumberjack**	**Plumber**
• Hair • Cut • Scissors • Trim • Stripe	• Airplane • Jet • Fly • Cockpit • Airport	• Forest • Tree • Cut • Saw • Timber	• Pipes • Drain • Sink • Toilet • Liquid
Cashier	**Jockey**	**Pastor**	**Mechanic**
• Clerk • Money • Register • Store • Check	• Horse • Race • Ride • Kentucky • Pony	• Church • Preacher • Minister • Priest • Seminary	• Automobile • Car • Garage • Fix • Goodwrench
Rock Singer	**Carpenter**	**Salesperson**	**Shepherd**
• Band • Play • Perform • Concert • Guitar	• Wood • Tools • Jesus • Make • Build	• Sell • Travel • Commission • Buy • Door-to-door	• Sheep • Staff • Lord • Flock • Baa
Photographer	**Truck Driver**	**Clown**	**Artist**
• Camera • Picture • Film • Develop • Take	• Road • Semi • Travel • Rig • Wheel	• Circus • Make-up • Laugh • Bozo • Ronald	• Paint • Draw • Palette • Color • Canvas

ACTS 19

What a Riot!

Early into his third missionary journey, Paul stops in Ephesus. He makes sure that everyone in the area hears God's Word during the two years he is there. The seven sons of Sceva learn not to use Jesus' name without having the authority to do so. Later, when Paul's teaching threatens the financial security of local tradesmen, the city is in an uproar.

(Needed: Flashlights without batteries, uninflated balloons, flat soda pop)

Announce that you're going to play a game. Form teams and give each team a flashlight—without batteries. When kids complain, tell them you forgot batteries, so you'll play a game with balloons instead. Give kids uninflated balloons and say: **The book here says we're supposed to tie balloons to our ankles and try to stomp on each other's balloons. Sounds kind of dumb, but let's give it a try.** Don't let kids blow up the balloons. Tell them you need to re-use them later. After giving up on this idea, serve some flat soda pop (air it out well in advance so there's no fizz). Then say: **This chapter starts with some people who thought they were disciples, but who didn't know about the Holy Spirit. Trying to be a Christian without the Holy Spirit is as pointless as trying to use a flashlight without batteries, playing with balloons without air, or drinking soda pop without fizz.**

DATE I USED THIS SESSION _____ GROUP I USED IT WITH _____

NOTES FOR NEXT TIME _____

_____

_____

1. What's the most supernatural thing that's ever happened to you, or that you've heard happened to someone else? (Point out that this chapter contains many supernatural events.)

2. As Paul was on his third missionary journey, he found some people who knew about the baptism of John the Baptist, but not about being baptized in the name of the Lord Jesus (vss. 1-7). What's the difference? (John's baptism only involved repentance, or turning away from sin. Being baptized in the name of Jesus also involves living for Him within the power of the Holy Spirit.)

3. What can prevent the Holy Spirit from working in someone's life (vss. 8-10)? (People can become "obstinate" and refuse to believe, even in the light of persuasive teaching about God's truth.)

4. What do you make of verses 11 and 12? (Even handkerchiefs and aprons that touched Paul somehow "carried" healing power to people who were sick or possessed by evil spirits. This sounds amazing, but it's evidence of the Holy Spirit's role in Paul's ministry.)

5. Yet the Holy Spirit is God, and not some magician's trick to be manipulated. How do the next few verses bear this out (vss. 13-16)? (The evil spirit refused to recognize the authority of those who tried to drive it out, and caused the man it possessed to beat them severely, leaving them naked and bleeding. This should serve as a strong warning against dabbling in occult practices.)

6. When it became known that the power of the Holy Spirit could not be faked or manipulated, what was the result (vss. 17-20)? (People had a new and instant respect for Christianity, confessing their sins and burning their occult materials.)

7. While some of the people in Ephesus became believers, others were threatened. Why (vss. 23-27)? (Craftsmen who sold idols were afraid that Christianity would put them out of business.)

8. **What happened when these men expressed their concern** (vss. 28-34)? (Pandemonium broke out. Paul's friends tried to keep him hidden, so the rowdy crowd picked on his friends instead. Every time someone tried to calm the people, they would chant their devotion to the goddess Artemis.)

9. **What do you think the crowd wanted?** (They wanted to create the impression that Paul [and Christianity] might be a threat to the city's lifestyle, and after the riot there was little chance for Paul to be taken seriously.)

10. **After chanting for two straight hours, what put an end to this hubbub** (vss. 35-41)? (The city clerk simply stated the rights of the Ephesian tradesmen as well as the rights of Paul and his friends. Then everyone went home.)

11. **Have you ever been part of, or seen, a crowd or mob that got out of control? If so, what happened?**

(Needed: Metal trash can and matches [optional])

Some people today are more like the Ephesian tradespeople than they would like to admit. When Christianity "invades" their personal territories, they feel threatened and react in defensive ways. Use the reproducible sheet, "Burn It, or Bow Down to It?" to get kids thinking about things that might keep them, and others, from following Jesus. Have kids share the symbols they drew on the pedestal and what they wrote underneath it, but don't have them share what they drew in the flames. If you can do it safely, burn kids' papers in a metal trash can to visually remind them of the need to get rid of anything in their lives that might keep them from following Jesus 100 percent.

BURN IT, or BOW DOWN TO IT?

In Acts 19:19, a bunch of Christians decided it was wrong to have books about the occult, so they burned them. The total value of the scrolls they burned was 50,000 drachmas. Each drachma was worth one day's wages—so that's about 140 years' worth of wages! There must have been a lot of people, a lot of scrolls, or both. In the flames below, draw some symbols, or write some words describing things that might keep you from truly following Jesus. This might include certain types of music, reading material, attitudes, movies, bad habits—anything you need to get rid of. Whether or not you actually "burn" these things is up to you.

Not everybody in Ephesus decided to torch scrolls. In fact, some of the people were upset that Christianity was threatening their income. One of the seven wonders of the ancient world—the temple of the goddess, Artemis—was in Ephesus. This brought in a lot of tourists who bought little silver Artemis shrines as souvenirs.

Most people you know probably don't worship Artemis. But what man-made gods (see verse 26) do they worship? On the pedestal below, draw a symbol to represent a "god" that people "worship" today. Underneath the pedestal, write some ways in which people would be threatened if millions of Christians refused to worship this "god." For example, the "god" might be "beauty." Executives at cosmetic and fashion companies might be threatened if people started buying less stuff; body building and beauty pageant organizers might be threatened if they had fewer contestants, and so on.

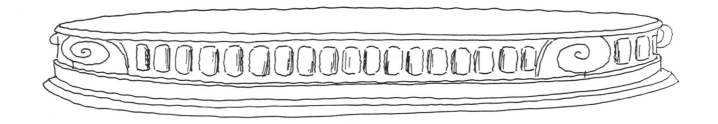

ACTS 20

These Good-byes Are Killing Me

After deciding to return to Jerusalem (19:21), Paul and his companions leave Ephesus and travel through parts of Macedonia and Greece, encouraging the believers there. Then they travel to Troas. The night before leaving Troas, Paul talks until midnight, resulting in the death (and resurrection) of one person. On his way back to Jerusalem, Paul has one last visit with the elders of the Ephesian church in the city of Miletus. They share a prayerful—and tearful—good-bye.

Make a copy of the reproducible sheet, "Snooze Break," and cut it along the dotted lines. You'll need six people to perform this impromptu skit. If you have fewer than six kids, give more than one part to the same person, and you can be the interviewer. Give the people who have the lettered parts (A-F) a moment to fill in their blanks. Don't let them know what the subject matter of the interview will be. Then have the newscaster "interview" the six people about their sleeping habits, having them answer by saying the things they filled in the blanks. Explain that this chapter in Acts contains one of the oddest sleeping episodes of all time.

DATE I USED THIS SESSION _____ GROUP I USED IT WITH _____

NOTES FOR NEXT TIME _____

_____

_____

(Needed: Map showing Paul's journeys [optional])

1. **Have you ever fallen asleep, or felt like sleeping, in an inappropriate place?** (At school; at church; while driving, etc.)

2. **After spending more than two years in Ephesus, Paul was moving on** (vss. 1-6). **He wanted to head back to Jerusalem. Why did he go there in such a roundabout way?** (If you want, look at a map showing Paul's missionary journeys. Instead of heading immediately toward Jerusalem, he went back through Macedonia and Greece to encourage believers there. He knew he probably wouldn't be in this region again, so he might have been saying good-bye to his friends in these areas. Also note his change of itinerary in verse 3—instead of sailing from Greece [probably Corinth] to Syria [north of Jerusalem], he went back through Macedonia to Philippi, and then down to Troas.)

3. **Can you identify with Eutychus** (vss. 7-12)**? Why or why not?** (Listening to Paul, he fell asleep, tumbled off a windowsill, and died. Ironically, the name Eutychus meant "fortunate." Fortunately, Paul brought him back to life, and then continued to speak until daylight!) **What's been your most embarrassing moment at church? Suppose Eutychus wrote a letter one week after this event. What would the letter say?**

4. **Paul was still in a hurry to get to Jerusalem, and his change of plans had slowed him down. He had already said good-bye to the disciples in Ephesus** (vs. 1)**, so when he came back through he didn't want to go back into town and do it all again. Instead, he called the elders of the church to come to a nearby town and meet with him** (vss. 13-17) **for what might be the last time. What did he have to say about the past they had spent together** (vss. 18-21)**?** (He wanted them to be assured that he had been completely open and honest with them.)

5. **What did Paul have to say about the current situation** (vss. 22-27)**?** (He wanted to make a smooth transition as he left. And though he fully expected to face suffering in Jerusalem, he was confident that God was still in control. Consequently, Paul would continue to try to "finish the race and complete the task" that Christ had given him. See Philippians 3:7-11; II Timothy 4:7.)

6. What did Paul have to say about the church's future in Ephesus (vss. 28-31)? (He wanted to prepare them for their own hard times. Paul knew that persecution and distortion of truth were in store for God's people. It would be the elders' responsibility to be prepared for this.) **What are some of the "savage wolves" that try to lead people astray today?** (New Age philosophies; cults; people who say that all Christians should be healthy, wealthy, and successful; etc.)

7. Based on verses 32 through 38, how would you describe Paul's work among the Ephesians and his relationship with them? (Paul was hardworking, honest, and giving. His relationship with the people of Ephesus must have been very close, as evidenced by their tearful parting. Prayer also played a key role in their relationship.)

8. When have you found it very hard to say good-bye to someone? What were your feelings as you left that person or group for the last time (or for a long time)?

People who have been forced to move away from friends, or who have seen parents divorce, might not agree that parting is "sweet" sorrow. It's never easy to say good-bye. And when the time comes, frequently the right words won't. Review the chapter and make a list of "Paul's tips for saying good-bye." Then write a group note or make a card to send to someone who has left your group, or to a missionary your church supports.

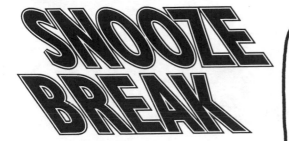

Newscaster:

Welcome to *Snooze Break*, the news show where we circle the globe to uncover people's oddest sleeping habits. *(Yawn.)* Excuse me. Today we've found five of the world's weirdest sleepers. Let's ask them a few questions. *(Yawn again, then interview each person. Feel free to ad lib.)*

A. 1. How many hours a day do you sleep?
2. In what room do you sleep?
3. Some people sleep in a bed. What do you sleep in?

B. 1. What do you wear to bed?
2. I understand you have lots of dreams. Who do you dream about most often?
3. And how would you describe these dreams?

C. 1. So, you walk in your sleep. How many miles do you typically walk in one evening?
2. What else, besides walking, do you do in your sleep?
3. You also talk in your sleep. What do you usually talk about?

D. 1. Some people count sheep when they're trying to get to sleep. What do you count?
2. Some people also have annoying habits when they sleep, like gnashing their teeth together. What annoying thing do you do in your sleep?
3. Some people sleep with a stuffed animal. What do you sleep with?

E. 1. The *Guinness Book of World Records* lists you as the world's worst snorer. When you snore, what do you sound like?
2. And how far away can people hear you snoring?
3. You once fell asleep in church. What were you doing?

A. 1. Any number from 1 to 24:_____
2. Any place in your house, besides the bedroom:_____
3. Any appliance, fixture, or piece of furniture in your house (other than a bed):_____

B. 1. Any two articles of clothing:_____
_____ and _____
2. Any person in this room:_____
3. Any adjective (descriptive word) starting with the letter "d":_____

C. 1. Any number:_____
2. Any activity that people do: _____
3. Something people your age talk about:
_____

D. 1. Something people collect:_____
_____
2. Something that annoys other people: _____
_____
3. Something people own: _____
_____

E. 1. Any loud or annoying sound:_____
_____
2. Any place in the world:_____
_____
3. Something people do in church:_____
_____

ACTS 21

You're Under Arrest

After a hard good-bye to the Ephesian elders, Paul sets off for Jerusalem, touching base with other believers as he goes. Repeatedly, and sometimes graphically, Paul is urged not to go to Jerusalem because certain arrest and persecution await him there. But Paul won't be talked out of it. And sure enough, his enemies try to beat him to death there. The only thing that stops them is his arrest (and chaining) by Roman soldiers.

(Needed: Dice; small candies or pretzels)

Play a game to see how much risk your group members are willing to take. Take turns throwing a die. Give individuals one piece of candy (like an M&M) or a pretzel for each dot they get—unless they throw a six. Once they throw a six, they have to give back all the loot they've collected. Kids can stop at any time and eat their winnings, or they can risk it all on additional throws. Play several rounds. See who can collect the largest amount. Today we'll see how Paul kept going, even though he knew it was risky.

DATE I USED THIS SESSION _____ GROUP I USED IT WITH _____

NOTES FOR NEXT TIME _____

_____

_____

1. What's one of the biggest risks you've ever taken? For the most part, are you a risk taker or a risk avoider? Why?

2. Paul had spent almost three years in Ephesus, which was about as long as he had ever stayed in one place. **What thoughts were probably going through his mind** (vss. 1-9)? (Paul probably had mixed emotions. He may have wanted to spend time building up the Christians wherever he went, yet he was also eager to get back to Jerusalem, his "home base." It must have been difficult to keep getting churches started and then leaving them behind. [Note: The "we" perspective in this account is not from Paul, but from the writer of Acts, Luke.])

3. If you had been traveling with Paul, **how would you have felt after the event that took place at Philip's house** (vss. 8-11)? (The Holy Spirit doesn't make mistakes. A prophecy of danger would certainly come true.) **How did the people there respond** (vs. 12)? (They were afraid for Paul.)

4. If you had been Paul, would you have gone ahead with your plans? (Let students respond.) **This had not been the first prediction of danger for Paul—it was one of several** (20:22, 23; 21:4). **How did it affect Paul's plans** (vss. 13, 14)? (Paul was no stranger to persecution. He had already "died" to himself in order to live for Jesus, so he was not scared away from what he felt was his ministry.)

5. Do you think Paul was going against God's will (to continue to Jerusalem after the prophecy by Agabus)? (No. Rather, he felt God's leading to go to Jerusalem [20:22-23]. The prophecy was just to alert him and the others to what was going to happen.)

6. Upon reaching Jerusalem, what news did Paul have for his friends there (vss. 15-19)? (He wanted them to know how God was working in all the places he had been—particularly among the Gentiles.)

7. What news did Paul's friends have for him (vs. 20)? (Thousands of Jews had become believers in Jesus as well.)

8. **What problem did Paul have to contend with right away** (vss. 21-26)**?** (Because Paul's work involved the Gentile people, rumors spread that he was rejecting Mosaic law. To dispel the rumor, Paul took part in a traditional Hebrew ceremony [which would have involved animal sacrifice] with a group of devoted Jews.)

9. **Paul's problems weren't over. Jews from Asia recognized him and began to level false accusations against him. What happened then** (vss. 27-31)**?** (Before anything could be done, a mob of angry people dragged Paul away and tried to kill him.)

10. **What kept Paul from being killed** (vss. 31-36)**?** (The Roman soldiers [likely 200 or more] sent to break up the disturbance arrested Paul, bound him in chains [as had been prophesied], and even had to carry him for his own protection.)

11. **The commander of the soldiers who saved him mistook Paul for someone else—an Egyptian terrorist leader. Do you find anything unusual in Paul's response** (Acts 21:37-39)**?** (Sometimes we tend to deny accusations so strongly that people suspect we have something to hide. But Paul focused on who he was, not who he wasn't. Also, Paul actually asked to talk to the people who had just tried to kill him.)

Paul's address to the crowd is contained in Acts 22. For now, use the reproducible sheet, "Don't Say I Didn't Warn You," to let group members consider if they would willingly go into a situation after being warned specifically of the dangers. When they finish, have them discuss any potentially dangerous situations they may have already experienced because of what they believed. If possible, have a few true stories at hand about people who "paid the price" for their faith—such as missionary Jim Elliot, who died at the hands of the Auca Indians in Peru. Then let students debate: "With proper planning, is it possible to avoid most dangerous situations and still lead a strong Christian life?"

Don't Say I Didn't Warn You

Warnings are frequently helpful things. If you're cruising down the road, and you suddenly see a sign that reads, "DANGER: BRIDGE OUT," you'd be pretty foolish to keep zipping along and pay no attention. But other warnings may keep us from doing things that would be pretty thrilling. Read through the "for instances" below and describe how you would be likely to respond in each case.

1 You're at an amusement park that has the scariest roller coaster in the state. Someone died on it (although he was goofing off) last summer. While you're standing in line, you notice a sign warning you of the dangers of this ride (you have to be so tall, can't have any heart conditions or epilepsy, don't wear glasses or hats, etc.). What do you do?

_____

_____

2 You're at the beach and it's a perfect day. You can't wait to go out into the surf. Then you see a lifeguard posting a sign warning that sharks were recently spotted in this area. What do you do?

_____

_____

3 You go along with some friends to a place that offers bungee jumping. Before you're allowed to jump, you're given a form saying that the management of the operation isn't responsible for any deaths or injuries. What do you do?

_____

_____

4 You have an opportunity to go to Haiti on a four-week missions trip this summer. Your mother warns you about all the health risks there and says you shouldn't drink the water. You hear on the news that there's some political unrest there. Then you read about all the voodoo worship that takes place in some of the villages. To top it all off, your best friend says, "Why would you want to waste your summer doing that?" What do you do?

_____

_____

5 A new kid moves to your school, and doesn't seem to make friends very easily. You're thinking about asking this new person to come to your youth group's next social event. But a friend says, "No way. Haven't you heard? This kid just transferred from a reform school. We're talking serious bad news." What do you do?

_____

_____

ACTS 22

Offensive Defense

Having just escaped death at the hands of an angry mob, Paul is allowed to address the crowd. He uses the opportunity to give his personal testimony, but the people refuse to be appeased. His Roman captors prepare to whip the truth out of him until he tells them he is a Roman citizen (who is exempt from such punishment). As an alternative, the Romans set up a meeting between Paul and his Jewish accusers.

Form pairs. Give each person a copy of the reproducible sheet, "Sending a Message." Have kids follow the directions, sitting back-to-back. See who can decipher the other person's message in the fewest guesses. In this chapter you'll see what Paul's message was to the crowd that wanted him dead.

DATE I USED THIS SESSION _____ GROUP I USED IT WITH _____

NOTES FOR NEXT TIME _____

_____

_____

Q&A

1. Have you ever had to give a speech or talk in front of a group of people? How did you feel before, during, and after your speech?

2. The Roman commander (see chapter 21) granted Paul's request to speak to the people. If you were facing the same angry people who had just tried to beat you senseless, what's the first thing you would probably say to them? What did Paul say (22:1-5)? (Since his adversaries were Jewish "purists," Paul began with a quick introduction to identify himself with them. But then he launched into the story of how he came to know and follow Jesus.)

3. Read Paul's testimony in verses 6-21. What did he choose to highlight? (His experience on the road to Damascus and a second encounter with the Lord back in Jerusalem.) If you were describing your own conversion to Christianity, do you think you'd tell your story as well as Paul told his? Why or why not? What information and/or experiences would you include?

4. Paul was addressing a huge group of angry Jewish people. Do you think it was wise for him to include the part about how Jesus had told him that he would be rejected by many Jewish people because they didn't know any better (vss. 17-21)? Explain. (It was almost certain to evoke a negative reaction, yet it was the truth. Paul didn't attempt to misrepresent facts in any way.)

5. Paul had boldly given his testimony. He had not held back anything, even at risk of personal injury. He had been faithful to God. So what was the result (vss. 22-24)? (The mob still wanted him dead. But an order was given to have him flogged instead.) Do you think God was unfair to leave Paul in such a situation, after Paul's faithfulness? Explain. (Some people may think so, but we often view things in the short run, not the long-run view that God has.)

6. Paul had allowed himself to be a target. Do you think he had given up caring what happened to him (vss. 25-29)? Explain. (Even though we can put our lives in God's hands, no one enjoys unnecessary suffering. Paul knew he was entitled to certain rights as a Roman citizen—including the right not to be beaten like a common criminal. And he didn't hesitate to claim those rights. Note that Paul was born a Roman citizen, and the commander had to purchase citizenship for a big price.)

7. **How did Paul's confidence in his citizenship help him (vs. 30)?** (The Roman commander released him and set up a meeting with the Sanhedrin to find out exactly what its members had against Paul. And again, Paul had the opportunity to speak to his accusers.)

8. **If the events in this chapter had taken place today, how do you think the news media would have covered it? What would be said and/or written?**

As a Roman citizen, Paul knew he had rights. Sometimes (as in this chapter) he claimed those rights. At other times he "waived" his rights to do certain things that might offend others (Romans 14). Discuss the following:

• **If you're a citizen of this country, what are some of your rights? How could you use the following rights to help spread the word about Christ, or glorify God in some other way: (a) the right to vote; (b) the right to travel to other countries; (c) the right to protest; (d) the right to buy and read the Bible?**

• **How might you need to give up one of the following legal rights in order to help spread the word about Christ, or glorify God in some other way: (a) the right to self-defense; (b) the right to spend your money as you please; (c) the right to take someone to court; (d) the right to read any book in the public library?**

SeNding A MeSsAge

DIRECTIONS:

1. In the grid below, write in a short message that you want to send your partner. You can position the message anywhere. Write it like this:

2. Don't ever leave more than one blank space between words. Your message can be as short or as long as you want. The longer it is, the harder it will be to solve.

3. Take turns calling out letter/number combinations. Your partner will tell you what letter is in that box, or if it's blank. (For instance, in the example shown, 2D would be the letter T; 3F would be blank.) Write your partner's message in the bottom box.

4. The first person to correctly guess the other person's message wins.

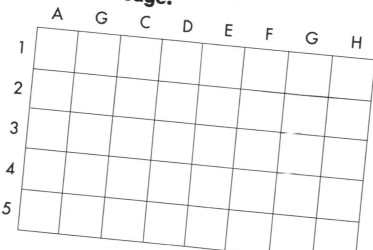

Your message:

Your partner's message:

ACTS 23

The Plot Thickens

Now Paul appears before the Jewish Sanhedrin, which has accused him of anti-Jewish teaching and defiling the temple (see 21:27-29). Paul wins some of its members over, but several of the others take an oath to kill him. When the plot is discovered, the Romans make arrangements to have him safely transferred.

Divide into two groups for an impromptu debate. Choose a topic on which opinion is about evenly divided. Here are some possibilities: Dog or cat—which is the better pet? Sausage or pepperoni—which is the better pizza topping? Guys or girls—which is the smarter sex? Have people get into their groups. Then tell them they have to take the *opposite* view of the one they hold. Give each group about five minutes to develop its argument. Then have each side present its case. This should be followed by a rebuttal from each team, and then closing arguments. As shown in this chapter, Paul knew that the Pharisees and Sadducees were divided over the issue of the Resurrection—and he used this fact to stir up a disagreement between them.

DATE I USED THIS SESSION _____ GROUP I USED IT WITH _____

NOTES FOR NEXT TIME_____

_____

_____

To help kids look at Acts 23 in a new light, hand out copies of the reproducible sheet, "The Perils of Paula." Then have kids read the actual account from the Bible and discuss the questions at the bottom of the sheet.

1. Can you think of any examples of people in positions of power who abuse their power? Why do some people abuse their power?

2. Paul was as well trained and qualified as any of the Jewish leaders. Yet he also knew and proclaimed the truth about Christianity, so the Jewish leaders tried that much harder to keep him under control. At this trial, what tactic did they use (vss. 1, 2)? (Physical force, by order of the high priest, Ananias—yet for no justifiable reason.)

3. Do you think Paul was justified in calling Ananias a name (vss. 3-5)? Why? (It is debated whether Paul actually didn't recognize the high priest, or was simply refusing to acknowledge his position due to his non-priestly behavior. Either way, Paul was correct in calling him a hypocrite.)

4. Because Paul was so knowledgeable about the religious beliefs of these people, he was able to cause a diversion (vss. 6-10). What did he do? (Knowing that the Pharisees believed in resurrection of the dead and the Sadducees didn't, Paul steered the conversation to that topic. Soon, many of the Pharisees were siding with him against the Sadducees. It seems as though Paul wanted this to happen so that he could be tried by a higher court.)

5. It must have been depressing for Paul to be rejected so often as he tried to tell others the truth about Christianity. What kept him going in spite of all the persecution he received (vs. 11)? (Paul never lost touch with God's will for his life. His encouragement came directly from God, so the approval of other people didn't seem so important.)

6. What is the strongest hatred that's ever been directed at you? How does it compare to what Paul experienced (vss. 12-15)?

7. If you knew that more than forty people had taken an oath not to eat or drink until they had killed you, how would you react? What plans would you make?

8. Tucked away in the pages of the Bible are a number of stories of unnamed young people who performed noteworthy, heroic actions. If you had the same opportunity to do what the kid in verses 16-22 did, do you think you would? Why or why not?

9. Thanks to the young man's efforts, arrangements were made for Paul to be transferred. **Do you think Paul felt safe as he was moved** (vss. 23, 24)? (Paul was probably more secure in God's protection than in the 470 soldiers assigned to protect him. But, to be truthful, knowing that forty or more assassins were "out there somewhere" must have been a little unsettling.)

10. A letter was written (vss. 25-30) **and Paul was safely transferred** (vss. 31-35). **Yet he was still awaiting trial. What do you suppose Paul prayed about while waiting for his accusers to show up?**

Paul's faithfulness to God didn't always have positive results. In this case, more than forty assassins were lying in wait for him. Your young people may not face such tremendous opposition, but they can probably identify a number of people or groups that they might not feel really friendly toward. Challenge each person in your group to make a list of his or her "enemies." This might include individuals, institutions, or groups—anyone your kids feel threatened by. Then read Jesus' words in Matthew 5:38-47 and spend some time praying very specific things for your enemies.

THE PERILS of PAULA

*P*aula looked straight at the jury and said, "Friends, I was just doing my job. I didn't do anything wrong."

At this, the chief prosecutor ordered that Paula be bopped on the head. Then Paula said to him, "Someday you'll get bopped on the head for this, you old hypocrite. You're putting me on trial here for breaking the law, but you just broke it by having me bopped on the head!"

Those standing near Paula said, "Now you've done it—you just insulted the chief prosecutor."

To this, Paula replied, "Ladies and gentlemen of the jury, I didn't realize that this was the chief prosecutor."

Then Paula noticed that half the jury members were blondes and half were brunettes. She was a blonde herself, so she said, "I am a blonde. And I'm convinced that blondes have more fun." After saying this, a dispute broke out among the jury, and they were divided.

This caused a great deal of turmoil. Some of the blondes stood up and came to Paula's defense. Then things really got out of hand. The judge quickly called a mistrial and had Paula taken back to her jail cell before she could be torn to pieces.

The following night, Paula's lawyer told her that this case would go all the way to the supreme court.

The next day over forty of those who wanted Paula dead made a vow not to eat or drink anything until she was dead. These hunger strikers asked the jurors to call another trial, so that they could kill Paula on her way to it.

Luckily, Paula's nephew heard about this plot and told her about it. Paula sent her nephew off with one of the jail guards to tell the judge about this plot.

When the judge heard of this plot to kill Paula, he decided to transfer Paula to another facility and have her tried by the state supreme court. So, he arranged for an armored motorcade—two hundred bodyguards, seventy police officers on motorcycles, and two hundred armed guards—to escort Paula to the new facility.

He wrote a note to the justice of the state supreme court:

> Your Honor,
> Greetings.
>
> This woman was seized by her enemies and they were about to kill her. She was rescued by police. We had a trial to find out what they were accusing her of, and nothing was concluded. Since her life is in danger here, we're sending her to you for trial. Her enemies will come your way to present their case.

So the armed escort took Paula to the new facility, and delivered the letter to the state supreme court judge. He ordered that Paula be kept in prison until the trial. Meanwhile, a lot of Paula's enemies grew very hungry and thirsty.

NOW READ ABOUT A SIMILAR STORY IN ACTS 23.

• How is the above story similar to the events found in Acts 23? _____

_____

• How is it different? _____

_____

• Why did Paula bring up the part about blondes having more fun? _____

_____

• Does this story help you understand any of the events in Acts 23 a little better? What questions do you have about the story in Acts?

_____

_____

ACTS 24

Here Comes The Bribe

Paul finally gets his "day in court" as Ananias, the high priest, brings charges before Felix, the governor of Judea. In spite of the false accusations brought against him, Paul's defense is sound. Yet Felix is slow to reach a verdict because he wants to receive a bribe. Paul is kept in a loose kind of house arrest for a couple of years until Felix is succeeded by Festus—Paul's next judge.

Use the reproducible sheet, "What's It Worth to Ya?" to see how far your kids will go to get clues to some puzzling riddles. Since your kids won't be seeing this, you don't really need to copy it. Read a riddle, and then have kids "bribe" you for clues. Give them just one clue at a time. Maybe they'll offer you some money, or food, or a promise to do you a favor. Once someone knows the solution to a riddle, have him or her tell you privately instead of announcing it to the rest of the group. This will keep the others in suspense longer. In order to solve the riddle of what to do about Paul, the judge (Felix) was hoping Paul would bribe him.

DATE I USED THIS SESSION _____ GROUP I USED IT WITH _____

NOTES FOR NEXT TIME _____

_____

_____

1. If life is like a courtroom, who do you most identify with at this point in your life: the person on trial, a lawyer, a judge, a member of the jury, the court reporter, an onlooker, or someone else? Why?

2. Paul had been hastily whisked out of town to avoid a secret plot involving more than forty people sworn to kill him (23:12-14). **But he had to wait around in protective custody until his accusers arrived. When they got there (five days later) and the trial began, what was one of the first tactics of the prosecutor** (vss. 1-4)? (He blatantly tried to "butter up" the judge.) **Can you think of any similar tactics (flattery, etc.) used by young people to try to get what they want?** (Trying to impress teachers; giving compliments, hoping to receive them in return, etc.)

3. When Ananias and his lawyer finally got finished trying to impress the judge, what charges did they bring against Paul (vss. 5-9)? Were they true? (If not outright lies, they were exaggerated. Riots had taken place in response to Paul's teachings, but he certainly didn't stir up the people intentionally. He had been accused of desecrating the Jewish temple, but it wasn't true. And he was a leader of the Christian movement, but "ringleader" was an inflammatory word.)

4. When people have gotten upset with you, how have they exaggerated the truth and made your actions sound worse than they really were? How have *you* done this?

5. What can you learn from Paul's presentation of his defense after these exaggerated charges (vss. 10-21)? (Point by point he calmly clarified the truth about each charge. It does little good to lose control or respond with nonproductive anger.)

6. Why wasn't Paul's case resolved right away (vss. 22, 23)? (Felix first said he wanted to wait for the commander who had previously rescued Paul to arrive and testify.)

7. But there was another reason. What was it (vss. 24-26)? (Felix was hoping Paul would offer him a big bribe. Later, in their frequent talks, Paul had several opportunities to present the Gospel.)

8. What are some ways that young people "bribe" each other or other people? (Pick up the tab in restaurants to impress the group; get gifts for others in an attempt to "buy" friends, etc.)

9. Since Paul never bribed Felix, the governor never got around to making a ruling on the case. Two years later Felix was replaced (vs. 27), and Paul remained in prison. What kinds of spiritual "jobs" do you tend to put off, hoping that someone will do them for you or offer you a "bribe" to do them?

Discuss whether group members would attempt the following "bribes."

• **Saying some nice words to a police officer who pulled you over for speeding.**

• **Slipping a few dollars to a foreign customs agent (at his request) to speed up your departure, thereby avoiding unforeseen delays.**

• **Buttering up a teacher in hopes of improving your grade.**

• **Giving a restaurant hostess a five dollar "advance tip" in order to get the best seat in the house for your big date.**

Then discuss: **Do you think it's always wrong to take or receive bribes?** Read Exodus 23:8; Deuteronomy 16:19; 27:25. **Can you think of anything you do that encourages others to bribe you in some way? If so, what should you do about it?**

What's it Worth to Ya?

RIDDLE #1

It has lakes, but no fish; forests, but no trees; and cities, but no houses. What is it?

Clues:

1. It's NEWS to me. [That stands for north, south, east, and west—but don't tell them that!]
2. Go ask Charles Atlas.
3. Fold it right there.
4. Have you checked your glove compartment?

Solution: A map

RIDDLE #2

The man who made it didn't want it; the man who wanted it didn't use it; the man who used it didn't know it. What is it?

Clues:

1. Don't Count me in. [A reference to Count Dracula—but let them figure it out!]
2. I'm scared stiff.
3. Let's bury the hatchet.
4. People are dying to get into one of these.

Solution: A coffin

RIDDLE #3

What comes once in a minute, twice in a moment, but not once in a thousand years?

Clues:

1. It's toward the middle. [Of the alphabet, that is—but don't let on!]
2. Some people follow the letter of the law, not the spirit.
3. Mickey Mouse and Marilyn Monroe would know.
4. Want some M&Ms?

Solution: The letter "M"

RIDDLE #4

In the town of Seville, there are two rules: (1) No man ever shaves himself—they all let the barber do it. (2) No man is allowed to grow a beard. There's only one barber in town, so who shaves the barber?

Clues:

1. 2, 3, 4, 5, 6, 7, 8, 9. [No one—get it? But don't give it away yet!]
2. The barber does own a razor.
3. The barber has a niece, but isn't an uncle.
4. The barber's husband is a real nice guy.

Solution: No one shaves the barber—she's a woman.

RIDDLE #5

You meet two guys who look identical. You ask if they're twins and they tell you they're not. But you find out that they have the same mother, and were born on the same day. You figure they must be lying, but they aren't. How is that possible?

Clues:

1. Think, think, think! [Three is the important number here—but that's for you to know and them to find out!]
2. See how they run!
3. Almost a homer.
4. They're three of a kind.

Solution: They're two members of triplets.

ACTS 25

All My Trials

Since Felix never ruled on Paul's trial before being replaced, Festus (the new governor) decides to hear the case. The Jewish leaders still want to see Paul dead, but don't get to carry out their plot. And even though Festus can find no cause to declare Paul guilty, Paul wants to carry his case to a higher court—before Caesar himself.

Make copies of the reproducible sheet, "Fend for Yourself," and give a copy to each member of the group. Have kids select which answer they think is the right one for each of the four cases. Divide into groups based on the answers given to the first case (all those who say "a" get together, and so on). Each group should defend the reasonableness of its answer to the rest of the group. After all defenses are given, see if anyone wants to switch groups before you announce the real answer (it's "a"). Do the same thing with the other cases as time allows. (Answers: [2] a; [3] d; [4] b.) Vote on who you think does the best job of defending his or her answers. In Acts 25, Paul gets another chance to defend himself against his accusers.

DATE I USED THIS SESSION _____ GROUP I USED IT WITH _____

NOTES FOR NEXT TIME_____

_____

_____

1. What are some injustices you've heard about in history class at school? Which one bothers you most?

2. After being picked up for causing a disturbance (21:33), **Paul had to keep presenting his case to a number of people: the crowd who had tried to beat him to death (21:40), the Jewish Sanhedrin (22:30), and Felix, the Roman governor (24:1, 2), to name a few. More than two years had passed (24:27). Put yourself in Paul's place; what thoughts are going through your head? How are you feeling?** (You're probably a bit frustrated at how slow progress is. Maybe you're tempted to reach a settlement soon, so you can be free again.)

3. **With the installation of a new Roman governor, Paul had to start from scratch. The Jewish leaders tried to get Festus to transfer the trial to Jerusalem (vss. 1-3). Why?** (They didn't just want Paul tried—they wanted him dead. [See 23:12-13.])

4. **But Festus wanted to hear the case. When he finally did, why couldn't he find Paul guilty (vss. 4-8)?** (The Jewish leaders couldn't prove their charges against Paul.)

5. **Festus wanted to find favor with the Jewish leaders, so at this point he tried to have the trial moved to Jerusalem. How did Paul prevent this (vss. 9-12)?** (Rather than letting the case revert to being a local religious matter, Paul appealed to a higher Roman court.)

6. **Why do you think Paul appealed to Caesar's court?** (Perhaps because if Paul could successfully defend himself in a high Roman court, other teachers of Christianity would have the opportunity to speak openly. This would also help the Romans to know the differences between Christianity and Judaism.)

7. **What opportunity came Paul's way in verses 13-22?** (The Romans were beginning to talk about him. When King Agrippa visited Festus, Paul was a natural discussion topic. Consequently, Agrippa wanted to hear what Paul had to say.)

8. What are some opportunities God has given you to share your faith with other people? (Discuss how sometimes people who we assume aren't interested may actually want to hear what we have to say.)

9. Why was Festus glad to have Agrippa around (vss. 23-27)? (Festus had no convenient way to explain why he was sending Paul's case to Caesar. Agrippa's presence would lend more credibility as Festus contacted the Roman leader.)

10. On a scale of 1 (least) to 10 (most), how scared do you think you would be in Paul's situation? How scared do you think Paul was?

Hand out blank sheets of paper. Have kids imagine that they have a chance to share the Gospel in front of a large group of influential (and a bit hostile) people. Give them a few minutes to draw anything they might be afraid of, or write down words to describe their fears. When they finish, let volunteers share their drawings and/or word lists. Then, as a group, make a list of "Fear Antidotes." As students list methods they use to overcome fear and brainstorm new possibilities (specific Bible verses, good books to motivate them, teamwork, etc.), write them down. Then at the next meeting hand out copies of the list they came up with. Refer to Paul and explain that if we focus on our fears, we aren't likely to be very effective. But when we learn to depend entirely on God, fear takes a backseat to speaking up for Him.

CASE 1

The Case of the Suspicious Sneeze
In 1894, a man named Fred Ott made history when he sneezed. Why?
  a. His sneeze was the first copyrighted motion picture.
  b. He broke the record for the world's longest sneezing spell—12 hours, 36 minutes, and 18 seconds.
  c. He was the first person to use Kleenex brand facial tissues.
  d. His sneeze was the first sound to be carried over radio airwaves.

CASE 2

The Case of the Strange Sculpture
Michelangelo (the artist, not the turtle) created many famous works of art, including the statue of David and the ceiling of the Sistine Chapel. One of his works, a sculpture called "Pieta" was unique among his many masterpieces. Why?
  a. It's the only work he signed.
  b. It's the only thing he sculpted out of gold.
  c. It's the only work he ever received payment for.
  d. It's the only work still standing in his hometown.

CASE 3

The Case of the Illegal Icelander
Olga Stensrud lives in a two-bedroom flat in Reykjavik, Iceland, with her dog, Fifi, and her cat, Fluffy. One day, she's sipping a cup of fresh-brewed coffee when she hears a knock on her door. When she answers it, a police officer says, "You're under arrest." Why?
  a. Coffee is illegal in Iceland.
  b. No single person is allowed to live in a two-bedroom apartment.
  c. No pets are allowed in apartment dwellings.
  d. It's illegal to own a dog in Iceland.

CASE 4

The Case of the Curious Court-martial
In 1974, Seabee Leon L. Louie made naval history by being the first person to be court-martialed (kicked out of the navy) for doing something to the commanding officer. What did Louie do?
  a. Kissed the commanding officer on the cheek.
  b. Threw a chocolate cream pie into the commanding officer's face.
  c. Impersonated the commanding officer.
  d. Told a nasty joke about the commanding officer.

ACTS 26

Agrippa-ing Testimony

As Governor Festus hosts King Agrippa, they both give Paul a hearing. Paul shares with them his past—both his Jewish upbringing and his conversion to Christianity. And even though Festus suspects Paul of being crazy and Agrippa is resistant to Paul's message, neither of the rulers feels that Paul has done anything for which he deserves to die.

(Needed: Wild clothes; marshmallows; phone book)

Show up in the wildest, most mismatched outfit you can put together. Solemnly give each person a marshmallow and explain that it is a rare, alien spore that kids should carry with them always because it has amazing, mysterious powers. Offer to read your text before you start discussing it; then start reading from the phone book. In other words, do whatever you can to get kids saying that you've gone crazy. Then explain that in this chapter, Paul was accused of being insane—but without good reason.

DATE I USED THIS SESSION _____ GROUP I USED IT WITH _____

NOTES FOR NEXT TIME _____

_____

_____

1. What was a story that you never got tired of hearing as a child? Do you have any stories that you still like to hear over and over? Why do you think some things get boring when you hear them too often, and others seem to get better and better? (Usually the stories that ignite our hopes and dreams can be new with each retelling. Other stories just get repetitive.)

2. One story that Paul never seemed to get tired of telling was of his conversion on the road to Damascus. This is the third time the account is presented in Acts. (See also chapters 9 and 22.) Why do you think Paul kept telling this story? (It showed the power of Jesus to change lives, and it provided the basis for everything Paul did from that point forward.)

3. Many of today's powerful testimonies seem to involve former Satanists, drug users, or other "big" sinners who received Christ. What kind of life had Paul led before converting to Christianity (vss. 1-5)? (He was a Pharisee—one of the people most committed to observing Jewish law. He had also been a major persecutor of Christians.)

4. What was the big difference between Paul the Pharisee and the Pharisees who refused to accept the teachings of Jesus (vss. 6-8)? (The Old Testament included numerous prophecies of God's future kingdom and the coming Messiah. Paul saw that Jesus had been the fulfillment of these predictions. The other Pharisees didn't.)

5. Sometimes as we grow, we hate to admit what kind of people we used to be. Was Paul this way (vss. 9-11)? Explain. (No. Paul was very open about his past. And it was exactly this contrast between "then" and "now" that made his testimony so effective. The more honest we are about our previous sinfulness, the more powerful will be our expression of Jesus' forgiveness of those sins.)

6. So Paul explained the vision he had (vss. 12-18) and how he had responded to it (vss. 19-23). Festus, the governor, responded to Paul's presentation with the comment that Paul must have gone insane (vs. 24). What can we

learn from Paul's reply (vss. 25-27)? (The existence of Jesus is historical fact. People don't have to agree with or respond to His teachings, but the facts can't be dismissed as meaningless.)

7. Most of Paul's comments had been addressed to King Agrippa. What was the king's response to Paul (vss. 26-28)? (In spite of Paul's logic, Agrippa didn't seem willing to make a personal decision. He sidestepped the issue, yet gave no indication that he could argue with what Paul had said.)

8. What do you make of Paul's response to King Agrippa's question (vs. 29)? (Paul didn't answer his question either, but makes a sincere statement of his wish that all those listening would become Christians someday, but not be put in prison for it.) **How do you feel about people who reject your Christian beliefs?**

9. Both Festus and Agrippa knew that the Jewish leaders wanted Paul dead, and they wanted the support of those leaders. Yet what conclusion did they reach about Paul (vss. 30-32)? (They found no reason to convict him of any crime. In fact, they would have released him if Paul himself hadn't wanted to present his case [and the message of the Gospel] to Caesar.)

The reproducible sheet, "Brush with Royalty," will put kids in a situation somewhat similar to Paul's imprisonment and contact with the leaders of the Roman Empire. When they finish, discuss their responses and point out how patient Paul was in this situation. Discuss: **Can you think of a situation or a person that you feel you've "put up with" long enough? How does it compare with what Paul went through? If you "lose patience" in your situation, what might the results be?** Point out that sometimes we must stop putting up with something—when we or others are endangered by sexual or other abuse, for instance. But most of the time our angry responses won't accomplish what patience could (see James 1:19, 20). Have kids pray individually or in small groups for the kind of patience Paul had, which can only come from God.

Oops. As you and your family happen to be driving through the new foreign country of Doomeria, you stop for gas. You decide to go for a short walk. Less than two minutes later, a young Doomster (a native) runs up with a policeman and says in perfect English, "That's the one! That's the person who took all my money." The policeman immediately drives you to the nearest prison.

(They apparently aren't big on civil rights in this country.) You are to be tried at once—before the king of Doomeria, no less. "At once" turns out to be in over two years. How would you respond to the king's following interrogation questions?

(1) How do you like it here in our country?

_____ You call this a country?! I call it a police state, you ruthless dictator!
_____ No comment. I demand to see a lawyer.
_____ It's very beautiful, though I can't say much for the honesty of its citizens.
_____ Other: _____

(2) What have you to say for yourself in regard to these charges?

_____ Hey, you're crazy, man. Like, you've got the wrong person.
_____ No comment. I demand to see a lawyer.
_____ The charges are completely false. I didn't steal anything.
_____ Other: _____

(3) We didn't find the stolen goods during your strip search. Do you have accomplices in our country?

_____ I'm with my family. We're close friends of the president of the United States. My mother is a senator and my father, uh, makes nuclear warheads for a living. And boy, will they be mad if I'm not returned to them soon.
_____ No comment. I demand to see a lawyer.
_____ I was traveling with my family before I was abducted by the policeman.
_____ Other: _____

(4) As you may know, Doomeria is an atheist country. If you share our view, things will probably go easier for you.

_____ Where do I sign up?
_____ No comment. I demand to see a pastor.
_____ I'm a Christian. May I tell you why?
_____ Other: _____

(5) What else do you have to say for yourself that might persuade me to release you?

ACTS 27

Tossed at Sea

Paul, still being held by the Romans, sets sail for Rome to present his case in Caesar's court. But it is late in the year to be sailing, and the ship encounters a terrible storm. Paul foresees the destruction of the ship, but the safety of the crew. And in the midst of fear, hunger, and despair, he provides their one source of hope. Consequently, when the Roman soldiers want to kill the prisoners to prevent any of them from escaping, the centurion in charge spares their lives.

Play "Train Wreck." Have students sit in chairs in two parallel rows facing each other, with about six feet of space between them (as if lined up on either side of a train car). Then have them count off and remember their numbers. One person is standing rather than sitting, and his or her goal is to find a seat. He or she may call any combination of numbers, and those people must rise and find a different place to sit. The standing person uses this opportunity to try to seat himself or herself. One person will be left standing each time. On occasion, the standing person may declare "Train wreck," when *everyone* must find another seat. ("Train Wreck" should lead into Paul's shipwreck.)

DATE I USED THIS SESSION _____ GROUP I USED IT WITH _____

NOTES FOR NEXT TIME _____

_____

_____

1. If you were in prison, how would you spend your "free" time?

2. In this chapter of Acts, Paul is still waiting to defend himself. But this time he has cleared all the lower courts and is looking forward to being transferred to Rome to present his case before Caesar. **How do you think you would have felt if you were Paul?** (Many of us might complain that we were still prisoners after a couple of years. But for Paul, presenting the Gospel in Caesar's courts was an opportunity he didn't want to miss. [See 25:12 and 26:32.])

3. **What do you think Paul's Roman captors thought of him** (vss. 1-3)? (Some probably thought his beliefs were odd. But he must have been respected, because he was allowed freedoms that might not have been available to others.)

4. Paul and his companions weren't having smooth sailing (vss. 4-8). Water travel became much more dangerous in the latter part of the year, and this was the time most people were docking their vessels until spring. In spite of Paul's vision of impending danger, **why did the Roman centurion in charge decide to go on** (vss. 9-12)? (More people were influenced by the opinions of the ship's owner and pilot.)

5. **Since most of the people seemed to respect Paul, why do you think they didn't listen to him at this point?** (It's not unusual for people to miss the connection between spiritual insight and practical experience.) **Do you think church leaders are worth listening to on subjects like sex or careers, or just on prayer and Bible reading? Explain.**

6. **What's the worst storm you've ever experienced? Describe what made it so memorable, and how you felt as it was taking place.** (Let group members discuss hurricanes, floods, or other severe storms they may have faced.)

7. The storm faced by Paul and his shipmates was so powerful and long-lasting that the crew and passengers gave up hope (vss. 13-20). **If you had been one of the crew, do you think Paul's attempts to provide hope** (vss. 21-26)

would have encouraged you? Explain. (It would take a great deal of faith to believe that he actually knew what would happen—especially when the storm showed no signs of relenting.)

8. **As the ship approached land, what part did Paul play in keeping the sailors safe** (vss. 27-38)? (He convinced the Romans to prevent crew members from trying to escape, and he provided a convincing argument for everyone to eat and find strength. And though Paul spoke with spiritual authority, note that these were practical helps, not just religious "crutches.")

9. **How was Paul rewarded for his help** (vss. 39-44)? (When the soldiers wanted to kill the prisoners to keep them from escaping, the centurion in charge would not allow it.)

10. **True to Paul's prophecy, everyone arrived on shore safely, though the ship was destroyed. Later, Paul wrote to Timothy and referred to people who "have shipwrecked their faith"** (I Timothy 1:19, 20). **What do you suppose he meant by the phrase? And what images do you suppose he had in mind as he wrote?** (Guide students in contrasting the physical shipwreck described here with the spiritual parallels for someone who "sails" against the will of God.)

The reproducible sheet, "Life Preservers," will call for group members to identify the things that threaten them during a crisis and the things they cling to when everything else seems to crumble around them. Let volunteers share what they've listed and which person in the drawing they most identify with and why. Close with a review of Psalm 23. Encourage kids to commit it to memory so they can recall it the next time they face a "storm" that seems to be too severe to endure.

LiFE PRESERVERS

We all face storms. Think of a time when you felt like your "ship" was sinking. Label the waves and lightning bolts with things that threaten you when times are rough. Then label the lifeboats and life preservers with the things you always depend on, or hang onto when everything around you seems to be going down with the ship. Finally, circle the person in this picture you most identify with.

Home, Sweet Rome

After the shipwreck described in the previous chapter, Paul and his companions wash up safely on Malta, where Paul performs several miracles. After a three-month layover, the group takes another ship and continues to Rome. There Paul meets with fellow Christians and interested Jewish leaders. Some believe while others remain skeptical. The book concludes with Paul under house arrest, doing what he's done all along: boldly preaching and teaching about Jesus Christ.

(Needed: Several rubber snakes, or pieces of rope)

Pair off for a snake toss. Give each pair a rubber snake (or a one- to two-foot length of rope). If you have a large area, have partners line up about two feet from each other and toss the snake back and forth, trying to catch it one-handed. Players should take one step backward after catching it. Any pair that drops it is eliminated. See who can get furthest apart. If you don't have enough snakes to go around, measure the furthest toss and have other pairs try to better it. If you're confined to a small area, see which pair can throw the snake back and forth the most times (one-handed) without dropping it in a sixty-second period. Ask group members what they think of snakes. Then tell them about Paul's experience with a snake in Acts 28.

DATE I USED THIS SESSION _____ GROUP I USED IT WITH _____

NOTES FOR NEXT TIME _____

_____

_____

1. What's the closest you've ever come to dying?

2. Paul and his shipmates—all 276 of them—had shipwrecked in a terrible storm, but had arrived safely on shore as God had promised (27:21, 22). All in all it was a pretty good place to crash-land, because the natives were friendly and helpful. But what happened immediately to disturb the group (vss. 1-4)? (Paul was bitten by a poisonous snake as he placed wood on the fire.)

3. The islanders seemed to believe what many people believe today—that if something bad happens, it is probably because the person is bad and deserves it. But when Paul didn't die, how did the people change their thinking (vss. 5, 6)? (They went to the other extreme and assumed he must be a god.)

4. What else did Paul do to show God's power to the islanders (vss. 7-10)? (He healed all the people on the island who were sick.)

5. What do you suppose the Roman soldiers thought of Paul at this point? (We don't know for sure, but it's hard to imagine them not being aware of God's power at work through him.)

6. After spending the winter in Malta, Paul's group continued toward Rome. (Malta was an island just south of Sicily, so they sailed north into Italy.) **As Paul got near Rome, he spent a week with some fellow Christians (vss. 11-16). How do you think it would feel to get together with fellow believers after being mostly among nonbelievers for several years? Have you ever gotten away from church or drifted in your relationship with God, then come back? How did it feel?**

7. Who did Paul spend time with next (vss. 17-23)? Why? (He met with the local Jewish leaders. They had no doubt heard the discussions as to whether Jesus was actually the Messiah. Paul, however, knew that he was often followed by those who fiercely opposed him, and he seems eager here to share his opinions before any of his opponents caught up with him.)

8. How did the Roman Jews respond to Paul's proclamation of the Gospel (vss. 24-29)? (As in most of the other places Paul had taught, the response to the truth about Jesus was mixed. Some were quick to believe. Others were skeptical. Others were reluctant to believe that God's blessing had also been given to the Gentiles.)

9. Since Paul hadn't done anything that the Romans considered criminal, he was allowed a good deal of freedom even though he was a "prisoner." How did he make use of his freedom (vss. 30, 31)? (Even while under arrest in Rome, he was able [and willing] to boldly talk about Jesus to anyone who would listen. We also know that he used this time to write letters to a number of churches to encourage them.)

10. The Book of Acts ends rather suddenly. What questions do you have about what happened after this? (Was Paul ever tried? Was he convicted or released? Did he ever appear before Caesar himself? Most scholars agree that Paul was eventually tried and released and that he continued his travels, perhaps to Spain. Tradition holds that he was eventually executed at the hands of Emperor Nero in about A.D. 67.)

Have kids circle their responses on the reproducible sheet, "Hearing Test." Discuss their answers, keeping in mind that there may be more than one "right" way to act on the items. Point out that understanding and action are the proof that we've really heard what God wants to tell us. As time allows, talk about actions kids could take in each of the situations described on the sheet.

"For this people's heart has become calloused; they hardly hear with their ears. . . . Otherwise they might . . . hear with their ears, understand with their hearts and turn, and I would heal them"
(Acts 28:26, 27).

How are your spiritual ears? Try this hearing test to find out. Circle the word or phrase after each item that best describes the way you'd probably react to it.

1. **The announcer on a TV commercial says, "Thousands are dying each week in drought-stricken North Africa. But you can help."**

| I hear and act | I hear and ignore | What'd you say? | Didn't hear a thing |

2. **Your youth leader says, "OK, that was a fun game, but let's get serious now. Come on. OK. Hey. All right. Hello?"**

| I hear and act | I hear and ignore | What'd you say? | Didn't hear a thing |

3. **At the mall you see a little girl, about two years old, standing by herself and crying loudly. Her parents don't seem to be anywhere nearby.**

| I hear and act | I hear and ignore | What'd you say? | Didn't hear a thing |

4. **Your pastor announces, "Our guest speaker this week is a man who spent 40 years ministering among the Muslim people. He has a special challenge for us."**

| I hear and act | I hear and ignore | What'd you say? | Didn't hear a thing |

5. **In the locker room after P.E. class, you hear two stronger kids pushing a third student around in the shower and calling the person "gay."**

| I hear and act | I hear and ignore | What'd you say? | Didn't hear a thing |

6. **A friend of yours says, "You're the only person I can tell this to. After this weekend, I'm not going to be around. Ever."**

| I hear and act | I hear and ignore | What'd you say? | Didn't hear a thing |

7. **While riding home from school on the bus, you suddenly have the feeling that God wants you to talk to the kid sitting next to you—a kid you don't know.**

| I hear and act | I hear and ignore | What'd you say? | Didn't hear a thing |

8. **Your mother says, "After the day I've had, I don't want to hear any more about what you don't have time to do. Just take out the garbage and do your homework."**

| I hear and act | I hear and ignore | What'd you say? | Didn't hear a thing |

9. **You and your friends pass a homeless man on the street. He holds out his hand and says, "Spare change for some food?"**

| I hear and act | I hear and ignore | What'd you say? | Didn't hear a thing |

10. **At camp, a speaker ends the final meeting by saying, "If you need God's forgiveness, if you need God's love, if you need God to help you make a difference in the world, come forward and stand with me at the platform—and we'll pray together."**

| I hear and act | I hear and ignore | What'd you say? | Didn't hear a thing |

ROMANS 1

No Excuses

Since Paul hasn't been able to visit the Christians in Rome, he sends them a letter. He encourages them to think about the huge difference between God's righteousness and people's sinfulness. We have no excuse, he says, for not discovering the truth about God. If nothing else, the wonders of creation should be proof of God's existence—and reason enough for our response.

Before the session, mess up your meeting place as much as possible. Overturn chairs, take pictures off the walls, dump crumpled paper on the floor, etc. When kids show up, pretend you don't notice anything unusual about your surroundings. Adapt to them as if things were always that way: for example, "sit" on an overturned chair by lying on the floor with your rear end on the seat. Start the meeting and make announcements, still ignoring what's going on around you. Notice kids' reactions. Then explain that in this chapter Paul talks about people who ignore the obvious evidence around them that there really is a God. Then straighten out your room enough to continue with the session.

DATE I USED THIS SESSION _____ GROUP I USED IT WITH _____

NOTES FOR NEXT TIME _____

_____

_____

1. Have you ever been promised something, but had to wait a really long time to get it? (Examples: a grandparent's promise to will something to you; a parent's agreement to let you date at sixteen, etc.) **How did you feel as you waited? How did you feel when the promise finally was fulfilled?**

2. **Paul could hardly wait to tell the Romans that the Messiah, promised to the Jewish people for hundreds of years, had finally come. How many bits of information about this can you find in Paul's letter before he gets to "Dear Rome, how are you doing?"** (In verses 1-6 Paul mentions his own title of "servant"; Christ's relationship to God; Christ's two natures and resurrection; what Christ provides for us, etc.)

3. **What did Paul want to get out of his friendships** (vss. 11-13)**?** (To help his friends grow spiritually, which caused him to be encouraged. He wanted to give of himself for the benefit of his friends.) **When you're hanging out with friends at church, do you ever talk about how your "Christian life" is going? What *do* you talk about? How about when you're outside of church?**

4. **Paul was eager to talk to everyone about Christ** (vss. 14-16)**. Does that seem weird to you? Why or why not? On a scale of 1 to 10 (10 highest), how eager are you to do this?**

5. **Why might a teenager be "ashamed of the gospel"** (vs. 16)**? If some parts of the "Good News" seem embarrassing to you, which parts are they?**

6. **What does it mean to live "by faith"** (vs. 17)**?** (We need Christ's righteousness to be saved; we can't be "good enough" on our own. Christ's righteousness is credited to our "account" when we place our faith in Him.)

7. **What kind of "sign" from God do you think it would take to convince skeptical kids at school that He exists? If they don't get that sign, does that let them "off the hook"? Why or why not** (vss. 18-20)**?** (No. If nothing else, the glory of God in nature is enough to show that He exists and is active in the world.) **What example from nature would you prefer to use as evidence that God is there?**

8. **If God's creation is evidence that He's there, why don't people believe in Him and obey Him? Is the problem the theory of evolution?** (That may be a factor, but the real problem is that people "suppress the truth" [vs. 18] because they'd rather do as they please than obey God. The theory of evolution wasn't prominent in Paul's day.)

9. **How do people in our culture worship "created things rather than the Creator"** (vs. 25) **today?** (They concentrate on appearance, possessions, sex, the results of human creativity, etc. They're obsessed with themselves.)

10. **If we don't choose to live according to God's standards, we have no standard to live by. What happens then** (vss. 24-32)? (People with no standards are victims of their own desires, including improper sexual preferences, greed, jealousy, murder, etc. It's hard to argue that anything is "sinful" when you claim there's no God to sin against.)

11. **Based on verses 26 and 27, do you think Paul would agree with the idea that many homosexuals have no real choice—that they are born that way rather than choosing that lifestyle?** (Note: Avoid giving the impression that homosexual relations are more unforgivable sins than the others listed. And don't let discussion turn into making fun of homosexuals. Some kids struggle with confusion in this area, and may need to know that they can talk to you about it individually without risking ridicule.)

Hand out the reproducible sheet, "If We're So Smart . . ." Have kids display their "man-made," imperfect versions of some of God's creations. Ask: **What's the best way you can help the non-Christians you know to understand that God is there and is to be obeyed and worshiped?** Point out that using logic and evidence from nature is good, but that living consistently as a Christian may be the most powerful evidence. Discuss how kids could do more of that in front of their friends and families.

If We're So SMART...

Some people think humans are so smart that they don't need God. They say people created God, not the other way around. Well, if we're so smart, how come we haven't figured out exactly how all the wonders of "nature" work—much less creating them ourselves?

People are creative—but we have our limitations. After each of the following questions, draw a picture that shows your answer. We've done the first one for you.

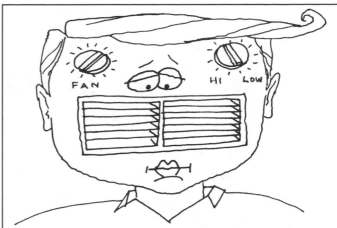

If the person who invented air conditioners had done the same with the human nose, what might your face look like?

If the person who invented computers had done the same with the human brain, what might your head look like?

If the person who invented the submarine had done the same with marine life, what might a goldfish look like?

If the person who invented garden hose had done the same with your circulatory system, what might happen if you got a cut?

If the person who invented light bulbs had done the same with the sun, what might a summer day look like?

Get off the Bench

Judgment is a serious thing in God's eyes. We should resist the natural impulse to pass judgment on others. God's "righteous judgment" is the only fair standard. If we set ourselves up as judges on the basis of our religious traditions or heritage, we risk becoming hypocrites.

Have five volunteers act out the skit on the reproducible sheet, "The Judge's Court." To add to the fun, first tell kids that they should stand up whenever anyone in the skit says, "All rise." After the judge exits, wait a few moments before telling kids they can sit down. Then ask: **How would you like to be judged by this judge? Why?** Point out that this chapter talks about the fact that none of us makes a good judge in areas that only God is meant to judge.

DATE I USED THIS SESSION _____ GROUP I USED IT WITH _____

NOTES FOR NEXT TIME _____

_____

_____

1. Has anyone ever judged you by the way you looked or talked? How did you feel?

2. Have you ever jumped to a conclusion about someone and found out later that you were wrong? What happened?

3. We tend to pass judgment based on appearances, and on behavior as well. **What's the big problem with judging other people's behavior** (vs. 1)? (We're all sinful, and to dwell on someone else's sin makes us hypocritical.) **Can you think of an example of hypocritical judging?** (A group of people might whisper about how *someone else* was "such a gossip.")

4. Some people say that we tend to criticize in others what we don't like about ourselves. Do you think that's true? Why or why not?

5. **What's the advantage of leaving judgment up to God instead of doing it ourselves** (vss. 2-4)? (God has a fair and truthful standard, and He is much more patient than we are. He wants people to repent, not just to "catch them in the act" of misbehaving.)

6. Do some teachers show favoritism to certain kids in your school? If so, how? **What do you think Paul means that "God does not show favoritism"** (vss. 5-11)? (Many people think their sins aren't as bad as others', so God will give them special treatment. The sins of "good" Christians are just as offensive to God as those of nonbelievers, so we should be sure to continually allow God to deal with our sins and our attitudes toward others.)

7. How many commands from the Bible do you suppose you know? Ten? A hundred? (Let kids respond.) **It's not enough to have a set of God's laws to live by. What else is necessary** (vss. 12-16)? (In addition to hearing and knowing the truth, we must obey it. This is why some people who might not know a lot about God may actually please Him more than someone who knows a lot but doesn't act on it.)

8. If you call yourself a Christian and say that other people should be more like you, what happens if you aren't a good example of being like Jesus (vss. 17-24)? (You mislead other people and blaspheme [dishonor] God.) **Does that mean you should keep quiet about being a Christian? Explain.** (You should identify yourself as a Christian—an imperfect one—and point people to Christ, not to yourself, as the perfect example.)

9. The Jews had the mark of circumcision to set them apart from other people (vss. 25-29). **What are some outer signs that some people take as indications of Christianity?** (Carrying a Bible; bumper stickers; pins; T-shirts; church attendance, etc.) **How well do these things prove someone's faith?** (They prove nothing. They may reflect a real faith, or they may be shallow substitutes for truly living for Jesus. To judge someone on such things can lead to misunderstanding and trouble.)

10. Rather than judging a nonbeliever for not being as "spiritual" as you are, what could you do for him or her? (Tell what Christ has done for you; invite the person to church; build a friendship and get to know the person better, etc.)

Give kids paper and pencils. Say: **Sometimes people display Christian bumper stickers and T-shirts with an "in your face" motive. "Christians aren't perfect, just forgiven" is true, but it might sound to a non-Christian like, "And you aren't—nyah, nyah, nyah." Try to design a T-shirt and a bumper sticker that you can wear "mentally" to help you remember not to judge other people. Your slogans should "stick to" you the next time you have the chance to pass judgment.** Let volunteers share their work. Then pray, asking God to remind each of you that He alone is the Judge.

THE JUDGE'S COURT

Characters:
Announcer,
Judge Waffler,
Crusty the Bailiff,
Mrs. Schnurtz,
Wendy

ANNOUNCER: It's time for *The Judge's Court*, the program that gives average people the chance to make each other look bad on television. Today we present "The Case of the Missing Milk Shake." Now entering the courtroom, here is your judge and mine, Judge Joseph Waffler.

JUDGE: Crusty! Crusty the Bailiff! You're supposed to say, "All rise." People are supposed to stand up to show how important I am.

CRUSTY: Oh, sorry, Judge. All rise! *(Everyone except JUDGE stands.)*

JUDGE: That's better.

CRUSTY: All sit! *(Everyone sits.)*

JUDGE: Now, what's this about a missing milk shake?

MRS. SCHNURTZ: She took my milk shake!

JUDGE: Hold it! You forgot to call me "Your Honor." That's to show how important I am.

MRS. SCHNURTZ: Sorry, Your Honor. My name is Mrs. Elizabeth Schnurtz, and—

JUDGE: Stop! The plaintiffs will speak only when spoken to. I'm the judge, so you have to do what I say! Crusty, I say everybody should have to stand up again.

CRUSTY: All rise! *(Everyone except JUDGE stands.)*

JUDGE: Good.

CRUSTY: All sit! *(Everyone sits.)*

JUDGE: Now, then. What's your name, young lady?

WENDY: Wendy, Your Honor.

JUDGE: Just "Wendy"? See here, young lady! In my courtroom, we use full names! Crusty, time to stand up!

CRUSTY *(wearily)***:** All rise! *(Everyone except JUDGE stands.)*

JUDGE: That's more like it!

CRUSTY: All sit! *(Everyone sits.)*

WENDY: Excuse me, Your Honor, but could we talk about the milk shake?

JUDGE: Order in the court! If I hear another outburst like that, I'll hold everyone in contempt! In fact, I already do! Now, what's this about a stolen milk shake?

ANNOUNCER: Uh, excuse me, Judge Waffler—but we're out of time.

JUDGE: What? You can't say that! Crusty, eject this man from the courtroom!

CRUSTY: But, Judge, he's the announcer. He has to say the part at the end.

JUDGE: Crusty, you can't talk back to me! Eject *yourself* from the courtroom! And take these people with you! *(CRUSTY, shaking his head, exits and takes WENDY, MRS. SCHNURTZ, and ANNOUNCER with him.)*

ANNOUNCER *(as he's being dragged away)***:** Tune in tomorrow to *The Judge's Court*, when we'll present "The Case of the—"

JUDGE: Crusty, make everybody stand up! Crusty, come back here! You're all sentenced to stand up for the remainder of your natural lives, or 99 years, whichever comes last! All rise! I'm outta here! *(He exits.)*

ROMANS 3

Everybody Gets an F

CHAPTER CHECK

While there may be certain advantages to bearing the label "Jewish" or "Christian," neither label is a key to righteousness. Paul's warning to the Romans is relevant to Christians today: "All have sinned and fall short of the glory of God." Only God can forgive our sins and declare us righteous.

OPENING ACT

(Needed: Large container of Jell-O and several quarters)

Before the session, make a large bowl of Jell-O or other gelatin. Put several quarters (or silver dollars, if you can find some) in the gelatin and let them sink to the bottom. Let the gelatin "gel" in the refrigerator. When the meeting starts, issue this challenge: **If you can remove these coins without touching the bowl, the surface it's on, or getting any Jell-O on yourself or on any object, you may have the coins.** Give kids a minute or so to try to figure out a way to get the coins under those conditions. But it's impossible. Make the connection to this chapter by pointing out that no one except Christ can be part of the human race without "getting sin on" himself or herself (vs. 9).

DATE I USED THIS SESSION _____ GROUP I USED IT WITH _____

NOTES FOR NEXT TIME _____

_____

_____

1. What's your favorite song—not for the tune, but for the lyrics? Why?

2. Do you have a favorite Bible verse or passage? If so, what is it?

3. What were some of the advantages to the Jewish people of being "entrusted with the very words of God" (vss. 1, 2)? (Knowing the truth; finding wisdom, comfort, courage, and peace; discovering that God created and loved them, etc.) **What are some advantages of owning a copy of the Bible today?**

4. What does "Let God be true, and every man a liar" (vs. 4) **mean?** (Even though people are unfaithful to God [in this case, the Jewish nation hadn't always kept up its end of the covenant with God], God never breaks His promises.) **Does that make you feel secure, guilty, or something else? Why?**

5. Have you ever taken advantage of the fact that a parent or teacher was "easygoing," or wouldn't punish you for every little infraction? What happened? If God loves us and forgives us when we sin, should we sin on purpose so He will be even more loving and forgiving (vss. 5-8)? Explain.** (In spite of His great love and forgiveness, God must judge sin. We should never take for granted His willingness to forgive us. Intentional, recurring sins pull us away from God rather than bringing Him closer to us.)

6. Paul makes it clear that "there is no one righteous, not even one" (vss. 9-18). And no one can become righteous by observing the Law (vss. 19, 20). So why did God give us the Law (and so much of it)?** (Because the Law shows us God's expectations, which make us aware of how far short we are of His standards.)

7. How can we get the righteousness we need (vss. 21-24)?** (When we believe in Jesus as Savior, God cancels out our sins with Christ's righteousness. That also allows God's Holy Spirit to work in our lives and help us toward righteous behavior that is otherwise impossible.)

8. Why did Paul want a "no boasting" rule about being righteous (vss. 27-31)? (Because in the righteousness department, nobody has anything to boast about. Neither Jews nor Gentiles could earn their way to heaven, since only faith in Christ can save us.)

9. Let's say you're an illegal alien living in New York City, working in a "sweatshop" clothing factory. The machinery you work with is unsafe, the pay is way below minimum wage, and the boss treats you like dirt. You can't complain because you're afraid of being deported. But one day you hear that everyone living in New York is hereby declared "legal," and is entitled to the same opportunities as everyone else. How do you feel? How do you think Gentiles felt about the announcement that they could become part of God's family?

(Needed: Trash can)

Pass out the reproducible sheet, "Sin Seating Chart." Let kids consider where they might belong in this "hierarchy" of sinners. Then explain that the whole seating chart idea is a fraud: **We'd like to think we're better than others, or that God is less offended by "little" sins like arguing than He is by "bigger" ones. But sin is sin, and none of us has anything to boast about.** Have kids tear up their seating charts and toss the scraps in a trash can. Encourage kids to consider whether they've been thinking of themselves as more "deserving" of God's grace than others are, and whether they've accepted the gift of Christ's righteousness.

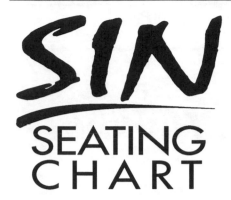

SIN
SEATING CHART

*Y*eah, yeah, everybody's sinned. But surely your little sins aren't as bad as some of those other people's. Where do you belong on the "great seating chart" of good and evil? If the "best" people get to sit in the front, and the "worst" sit in the back, where is your seat? Mark it on this chart.

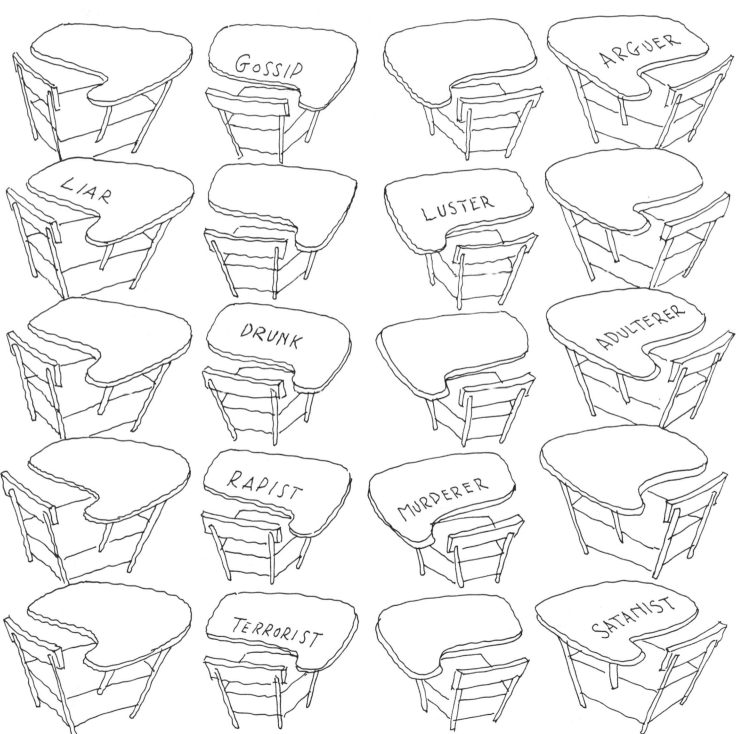

ROMANS 4

Our Dad, Abraham

Paul uses Abraham as an example of how God declares people righteous by means of their faith. Surely if righteousness required a certain level of obedience, Abraham would have been a model to follow. Yet it was Abraham's belief in God—not his resulting obedience—which "was credited to him as righteousness." Justification is received through faith, not works.

(Needed: Assortment of packaged snacks)

Bring an assortment of prepackaged snacks (Twinkies, snack-sized chips, cookies, candy bars, etc.). Pass them, still wrapped, to kids. Before they can start eating, though, ask: **How do you know that it's safe to eat this food? What if somebody at the factory had a grudge against the company and put rat poison in that food? What if someone tampered with it while it was on the shelf? What if I did something to it before giving it to you?** If kids still want to eat the food, point out that they apparently have faith in somebody. Is it the manufacturer? The grocer? The public? You? If they don't want to eat it, ask whether their faith in one of these has wavered. Then point out that faith is the subject of this chapter.

DATE I USED THIS SESSION _____ GROUP I USED IT WITH _____

NOTES FOR NEXT TIME _____

_____

_____

1. What living person is the best example of what you think a Christian should be? Why would you select that person?

2. When Paul wanted to discuss faith, he used an example his audience would respect—Abraham. God had brought the Jewish nation into existence through Abraham. What made him such a good example (vss. 1-3)? (Though he wasn't perfect, he was an obedient servant who did what God instructed, and showed great faith that God could do anything.)

3. What does it mean that Abraham's belief in God "was credited to him as righteousness" (vs. 3)? (Abraham lived hundreds of years before Jesus, and even before the Law had been given to Moses. Abraham trusted God in spite of those "handicaps," and God counted that trust as righteousness.)

4. Does your relationship with God usually feel more like (a) that of an employee and a boss; (b) that of a child and a parent; or (c) that of a student and a teacher? Why? If it ever feels like an employee/boss relationship—in which you put in a certain amount of work and expect to be "paid" with eternal life—what would be a better way to relate to God (vss. 4-8)? (The works we do should be a voluntary, happy response to becoming a Christian. Spiritual "discipline" isn't a contractual agreement with God. He doesn't "owe" us anything in return for our little efforts. We should put our faith in God and gladly receive the forgiveness [and other gifts] that He freely offers.)

5. The question keeps coming up throughout the New Testament about whether the Gentiles are as welcome to become Christians as the Jews are. What did Paul have to say here—even as he used Abraham as an example (vss. 9-17)? (The Jewish people knew that Abraham was the first to be given the mark of circumcision as a sign of devotion to God. Yet Paul points out that God considered Abraham to be righteous because of his expression of faith, which was *before* his circumcision. Therefore, any uncircumcised Gentile could express the same faith in God and be declared righteous.)

6. What did Abraham do that showed he had such faith in God (vss. 18-22)? (He believed that God would honor His promise to give Abraham a son—even though his wife, Sarah, was ninety years old and shouldn't have been able to bear children.) **In what kind of tough situation could a teenager show that kind of faith today?** (Example: Believing that God will take care of him or her in spite of a family breakup.)

7. What's one promise from God that you find hard to believe sometimes? (That He'll provide all we need; living forever in heaven, etc.)

8. How can we be "credited" with righteousness, as God did with Abraham (vss. 23-25)? (We must simply put our faith in God and believe that He raised Jesus from the dead in order to save us from our sins.)

9. Would you rather trust God to give you what He feels is best for you, or would you prefer more of a contract ("If I do this, You'll do that," etc.)?

The reproducible sheet, "Abe 'n' Me," helps kids contrast their faith with Abraham's. When they finish, discuss answers as kids are willing. Point out that for Abraham, his relationship with God was not just one compartment of his life. Rather, it affected everything he did. Challenge kids to "bring God with them" everywhere this week, too.

Abe&Me

Find it hard to relate to
Abraham's story? Maybe God hasn't promised
that you'll be the parent of a great nation. So
bring Abraham's experience "home"
to your world by comparing these parts of
his life with yours.

ABRAHAM: "I accepted
an outward sign—
circumcision—to show
that I believed in God. Are
there any outward signs—
clothes, behavior, or
whatever—that you have
because you belong to God?"

_____
_____
_____
_____
_____
_____
_____

"When it came to my
relationship with God,
my belief in God was
credited to me as
righteousness. What's
the basis of your
relationship with God?"

_____
_____
_____
_____

"I really had to exercise
my faith to believe that
Sarah and I would have
a child—even though I
was 100 years old.
What's one time when
you've shown very
strong faith in God?"

_____
_____
_____
_____

"I guess you could say I had a
spiritual influence on others.
The agreement God made with
me was passed down to many
future generations. What's one
way that you've been a
positive influence on another
person spiritually?"

_____
_____
_____

"I remember the hardest
thing God ever expected
of me. He asked me to
sacrifice my only son,
Isaac, on Mount Moriah
(at the last minute He
provided a ram to
sacrifice instead). What's
the hardest thing that you
feel God has expected of
you?"

_____
_____
_____
_____
_____
_____

"No, I wasn't perfect. My
faith slipped sometimes
when I was afraid—like the
times I lied about Sarah
being my wife, in order to
protect myself. And I tried
to hurry God along by
having a son with a woman
other than my wife. What
would you say your biggest
slip-ups have been when it
comes to trusting God?"

_____
_____
_____
_____
_____
_____
_____

ROMANS 5

Peace, Man

Thanks to the righteous standing we have before God because of Jesus' sacrifice, we can have peace with God. We no longer have to fear God's wrath for our sins. Death, the result of sin that was brought into the world by Adam, can be replaced with life. People's sins are many, but God's grace is even greater.

Before the session, cut the four situations from a copy of the reproducible sheet, "Hey, Aren't You . . . ?" Give the slips to four volunteers. Each should read his or her situation aloud, then act out what he or she might do next. You (or another volunteer) should play the part of the famous person in each ensuing conversation. Applaud the roleplays. Then ask: **How would you feel in a situation like that? Why? If you feel that way around a celebrity, how do you feel as you worship a holy, all-powerful God?** As this chapter points out, we should have peace with God.

DATE I USED THIS SESSION _____ GROUP I USED IT WITH _____

NOTES FOR NEXT TIME_____

_____

_____

1. What's the most uncomfortable you've ever been in a group of people? Why?

2. On a scale of 1 (least) to 10 (most), how much peace do you feel in your relationship to God? Explain.

3. What gives Christians the right to feel at peace in their relationships with God (vss. 1, 2)? (They have been "justified by faith" [declared righteous by God through their belief in Jesus].) **Does that mean that we can be "good buddies" with God?** (We have the freedom to draw near to Him and get to know Him better, yet we shouldn't take lightly the relationship we have with Him. Just because we no longer need to fear His wrath doesn't mean we don't need to give Him our respect. We are still sinful creatures who owe Him our reverence.)

4. How would you feel if you'd just lost your arm in an accident, and somebody told you to "rejoice in [y]our sufferings" (vs. 3)? (Probably angry. The point of Paul's statement is not that we should be glad *for* tragedies, but that we should learn to be glad *in* the midst of pain—because we can get qualities like perseverance, character, and hope as we trust God to help us through.)

5. Do you think you'd be willing to die in place of someone else? If so, who? And under what conditions? (Contrast answers with verses 6-9. Jesus died for each of us—sinners who deserved the penalty of death. His sacrifice on our behalf is without precedent or equal.)

6. Have you ever had a fight with a friend, but then made up? How did the "making up" process work? (Compare the use of the word *reconciliation* in friendships with its use in verses 9-11.)

7. Is it possible to lead a totally sinless life (vss. 12-14)? Explain your answer. (Only Christ has done that. The rest of us, because of Adam's sin, have been born with sinful natures.)

8. Do you think it's unfair to get blamed for the actions of Adam and Eve? Would you have done better in their place (vss. 15-19)? (We may think we might have done better than Adam and Eve—until we see how quick we are to sin even after knowing what God has done for us. But just as we share in Adam's sin, we also share in Jesus' grace and relationship to God.)

9. **How did God help us see more clearly our sinfulness, and then our forgiveness (vss. 20, 21)?** (The Law was given as a barometer of God's expectations for mankind. No one could fully obey it, which showed the need for another way to be restored to God's favor. Jesus' sacrificial death did for us what the Law never could.)

10. **When was the last time you thanked God for the peace and forgiveness He's made possible for you? How could you work this into the way you usually pray?**

(Needed: A ladder [optional] or a drawing of a ladder)

Read verses 3 and 4 again. Display a ladder (or just a drawing of a ladder) to illustrate the steps in the verses. Ask: **How could suffering get you to the next rung, perseverance (sticking with it)? How could learning to persevere build you up to the next rung, character? How could having the kind of character God wants you to have boost you up to hope?** (The more you trust God during suffering, the more you learn patience; the more you're willing to stick with it, the more time and effort you're willing to put into developing qualities like faith; the more faith you have, the stronger your hope—your certainty that you have eternal life. **Can you "fall off" this ladder?** (We all have shortcomings of character and lose hope from time to time.) **Do sufferings ever end?** (No, but our response time to shift from "suffering" to "perseverance" can become shorter.) **Where are you on this ladder today?**

HEY, AREN'T YOU...?

S I T U A T I O N 1

You're camping alone in the woods in the state of Maryland. Suddenly a man walks out from behind a tree. You recognize him; it's the President of the United States! He explains that he was out hiking, got separated from the Secret Service, and is lost. He hopes you can direct him back to Camp David. And in the meantime, could he have some of that hot chocolate you're making?

S I T U A T I O N 2

You're trying to call a friend who moved away last year. But you dial the phone incorrectly and a stranger answers. Suddenly you recognize her voice and realize that she's not exactly a stranger after all; she's the star of your favorite TV sitcom! You blurt out that you dialed the wrong number, but that you're a big fan of hers. She doesn't seem angry. There's a pause on the line, as if she's waiting for you to continue the conversation.

S I T U A T I O N 3

You're in a fairly nice restaurant with a date. You get up to use the rest room. While you're combing your hair, somebody walks in and uses the mirror, too. You turn to glance at this person, and are shocked to see that it's your favorite singer! Suddenly you recall hearing on the radio that this person is in town. "Hi," the singer says, seeing you staring. "Can you tell me where to find some decent barbecued ribs in this town?"

S I T U A T I O N 4

You're supposed to meet a friend on the observation deck of a very tall skyscraper. You wonder why there are some people with TV cameras outside the building as you walk into the building's lobby. You step into an elevator, and it begins the long climb. There are two older women and a man in the elevator with you. When you turn to look at them, your mouth falls open. One of them is the Queen of England! The other woman must be her secretary, and the man looks like some kind of guard. You knew the Queen was visiting the city, but didn't think you'd see her. Just then the elevator shudders and grinds to a stop, halfway between floors. You're stuck.

ROMANS 6

Sorry, I'm Dead

What a change knowing Jesus makes in a person's life! Paul says your old self dies—is crucified and buried—and replaced by a new self. The greater a person's sin, the more obvious Jesus' love and forgiveness is. Now, instead of being slaves to sin, we can be "slaves" to righteousness. Instead of expecting spiritual death, we can look forward to eternal life.

(Needed: Modeling clay)

Give each person a hunk of modeling clay. Give each person three to five minutes to turn the clay into a sculpture of a person, animal, or building. Let kids show their creations briefly. Then have each group member pass his or her sculpture to the person on his or her right. Say: **You have two minutes to turn the sculpture you've been given into one that looks just like the first one you did. Go!** After two minutes, see how kids did. What was hardest about remolding the sculptures? Then point out that this chapter describes changes that are even more radical than the ones kids made in their sculptures—changes God wants to make in us.

DATE I USED THIS SESSION _____ GROUP I USED IT WITH _____

NOTES FOR NEXT TIME _____

_____

_____

1. True or false? (a) People who are blind never have lustful thoughts because they never see suggestive movies or magazine ads; (b) there is no theft in countries that cut off the hands of people who are caught stealing. (Point out that while ignorance or harsh penalties may cut down on wrongdoing, they won't eliminate sin.)

2. What would be the reaction of a dead person to each of the following temptations: (a) a stack of CDs on the counter of a record store with no one at the cash register; (b) a pornographic magazine that comes to your mailbox by mistake; (c) the chance to get revenge by putting sugar in a "snobby" kid's gas tank?

3. If you're a Christian, what should be your attitude toward sin (vss. 1-4)? (Our new relationship with Jesus should make us different people. It should be as if we've "died to sin." Dead people can't sin. And if our "old self" is dead, then we should act accordingly.)

4. Think about question 2 again. In each case, what desires would you have to "count yourself dead to" in order to react as a dead person would?

5. As Jesus showed us, after death comes a resurrection. When we believe in Jesus and "die" to sin, in what sense do we become alive again (vss. 5-10)? (We discover real freedom as we get an eternal life [starting now] to live for Jesus. Now, rather than being hopeless slaves to sin, we need no longer fear death.)

6. If we've "died to sin," does that mean we'll never sin again? (Most Christians would agree that it's difficult to completely overcome the old and sinful nature that once enslaved us. We should keep making progress, though.)

7. Look at verses 11-14. If you were going to make up a "living will" donating your body parts for the Lord's use in *this* life, how would you expect Him to use your brain, your eyes, hands, feet, etc.?

8. Why be "slaves to righteousness" (vs. 18)? Why not stop being a slave to sin and just become master of your own life (vss. 15-18)? (Everyone serves somebody. Those who think they're running their own lives are denying God His rightful place and serving their sinful natures. It's just as important to become devoted to righteousness as to stop being a slave to sin.)

9. How do some sins today result in death (vss. 19-21)? (All sin leads to spiritual death, but many sins are physically dangerous as well: drinking and driving, sexual activity that might result in AIDS or abortion, drug use, etc.)

10. How could you celebrate the Good News in verses 22 and 23?

(Needed: Scissors)

Have kids cut the "death" and "rebirth" certificates from the reproducible sheet, "The End and the Beginning." Individuals should fill these out. These certificates record the same event—receiving Christ as Savior. Dates can be as approximate as kids want them to be—since the fact is much more important than the date. This may be a good opportunity to summarize how to become a Christian for those who aren't sure they've been "reborn." "Cause of death" should reflect the process of "dying with Christ." "Earthly spiritual parents" might be any people who helped kids through the process of becoming Christians. Let volunteers tell how they filled out their certificates. Encourage kids to take these with them as reminders of their "deaths" and "new lives."

THE END AND THE BEGINNING

Death Certificate

This is to certify that

_____
(Name)

died to sin on approximately this date:

_____

Cause of death:

_____

This death to sin will be marked by the following symptoms:

_____
_____

Signed:

_____
(Deceased)

Rebirth Certificate

This is to certify that

_____
(Name)

came to life in Christ on approximately this date:

_____

Earthly spiritual parent(s):

_____

This rebirth will enable the undersigned to do good works like the following:

_____
_____

Signed:

_____
(Child of God)

ROMANS 7

I'm Just a Guy Who Can't Say No

Paul continues to contrast the limits of the Law with the freedom and salvation made possible by Jesus. He gives some personal examples. As well trained as he'd been under the Law, he knew from experience that it lacked the power to prevent him from doing what he knew he shouldn't. His experience with the Law convinced him of the need for a Savior.

(Needed: Prize [optional])

Hand out copies of the reproducible sheet, "All Torn Up." Have kids compete to see who can tear out the spiral (in one unbroken piece) first. This should be pretty frustrating. If you like, award a prize to the person who finishes first (or the person who's furthest along after three minutes). Then explain that this chapter is about one of life's biggest frustrations— wanting to do the right thing, but doing the wrong thing instead, over and over.

DATE I USED THIS SESSION _____ GROUP I USED IT WITH _____

NOTES FOR NEXT TIME _____

_____

_____

Q&A

1. If you were "going" with someone of the opposite sex, would you be jealous if a "competitor" flirted with him or her? How about if a competitor went out with him or her? Why or why not?

2. Why does Paul talk about death and remarriage in verses 1-4? What's his point? (He wants to explain that because Christians have "died" to sin and to the law of Moses, they are free to become alive to Christ. Remarriage after the death of a spouse was perfectly acceptable. Christians are eligible for a new relationship with Christ.) **How is your relationship with Jesus like marriage? How is it different?**

3. If the Law is no longer our main guiding factor, what is (vs. 6)? (We should submit to the Holy Spirit, who can help us obey God more fully than written rules could.)

4. One day your mom says, "Stay out of that six gallons of choco-marshmallow-macadamia ice cream that's in the freezer. It's for company." Before she said that, you didn't know there was anything but celery in the house. How is that like Paul's point in verses 7-13? (This was the tendency of the Law—to reveal that certain things were wrong and should be avoided. Yet that provided new opportunities for people to learn to sin.)

5. When people are stopped for speeding, do they tend to blame themselves, the police officer, the car, a sign, the weather, or the law? (Many people blame anyone and everything except themselves.) **If the cause of sin wasn't actually the law of Moses, what *was* the problem** (vss. 14-20)? (People are sinful by nature and can't totally control their actions on their own.)

6. Can you think of a bad habit you wanted to give up, but just couldn't seem to? Or a time when you wanted to do something good, but kept getting sidetracked and never got around to it? What do you think the reason was? (Compare with Paul's frustration expressed in verses 18 and 19.)

7. If you just spend enough time reading the Bible, won't your tendency to sin go away (vss. 21-23)? Explain. (Not necessarily. Even as Paul could "delight in God's law," he couldn't always summon the will to do what he knew was right.)

8. Paul didn't like being out of control of his actions. What was his solution (vss. 24, 25)? (It involves God and our new lives in Christ [vs. 25], but Paul's solution isn't detailed until Romans 8. There we see that the power of the Holy Spirit is more than enough to help us deal with any temptation that comes along.)

9. On a scale of 1 (least) to 10 (most), how strongly do you identify with the inner struggle Paul describes in verses 15-24?

10. What kinds of problems do you like to deal with on your own? When do you decide it's time to get help? (Many kids are fiercely independent and may be reluctant to receive assistance from others—perhaps even from God.)

Give kids paper and markers. Say: **How do you feel when you want to do the right thing, but just can't seem to? Draw something on this paper to show that feeling.**

When kids finish, let kids show and explain their pictures if they want to. Ask: **Where do you think God is when you feel that way? Why?** Point out that Romans 8 gives some answers to the problems raised in chapter 7. If you won't be studying Romans 8 soon, point out passages like Philippians 1:6: "Being confident . . . that he who began a good work in you will carry it on to completion until the day of Christ Jesus." Encourage kids with the fact that each time they resist temptation, they grow stronger and better able to resist next time.

ALL TORN UP

Directions: Tear this spiral along the lines. You must make one continuous tear. If you rip the spiral so that it's in more than one piece, you'll be disqualified.

ROMANS 8

Stuck on You

After spending several chapters detailing the limitations of the law, Paul comes to a powerful conclusion. Those who are in Christ are no longer condemned. We can choose to follow the leading of the Holy Spirit rather than that of our sinful desires. We are children of God. The Spirit helps us pray. We are more than conquerors. And nothing can separate us from the love of Christ.

(Needed: Team prize [optional])

Form two teams. Line them up as if to play tug-of-war, but without a rope. They must pantomime a tug-of-war. Every so often, however, you'll call out the name of a kind of cord, and kids must pull as if they're pulling that kind of cord. They should fall down when they think they've reached the breaking point of that particular kind of cord. Each person must decide when that point is reached; no signals are allowed. Here are some cords you can call out: thread; kite string; rubber band; human hair; fish line; water-skiing rope; chain of paper clips; telephone cord, etc. If you like, award a prize to the team whose members do the best job of falling down at the same time. Then point out that in this chapter Paul talks about a bond that no one can break.

DATE I USED THIS SESSION _____ GROUP I USED IT WITH _____

NOTES FOR NEXT TIME _____

_____

_____

1. Have you ever worried about an event that was coming up, but at the last minute discovered that it had been canceled? How did you feel?

2. How do you feel about the news in verses 1-4? Why? (Because we're no longer under the Law, wc can feel a great sense of freedom because God doesn't condemn us.)

3. How can we "tune in" to know what the Holy Spirit wants for us (vss. 5-8)? (Like tuning a radio, it depends on how we "set" our minds. Some people are "set" on their own selfish desires. We can find out through studying the Bible what God's Spirit wants in general and ask Him for more specifics, but not much will happen to our attitudes and actions until we "set" our minds on what we know of what He wants.)

4. Why would following the Holy Spirit's guidance give you peace (vss. 5-13)? (Because you won't be trying to fight God and what He wants for you.) Have you ever felt as if you were fighting with God or resisting something He wanted you to do? How did it feel? What was the result?

5. If we're "controlled" by the Spirit (vs. 9), are we like robots? And if we're controlled, how could it even be possible to obey the sinful nature (vss. 12, 13)? (When we belong to Christ, we're no longer controlled by our old natures. But God doesn't force obedience from us. He wants us to submit to the "control" that is His right. When we do, He helps us become all we're meant to be, not less than we could be.)

6. Look at verses 14 and 15. If you haven't received the "Spirit of sonship," what might you be afraid of? (Approaching God; being punished by God; death, etc.) Do you feel like a "child" of God (vss. 16, 17)? In what ways do you treat God as you would an earthly father?

7. As a child of God, shouldn't you get to skip the problems of life that other people face (vss. 17-25)? Explain. (We won't get the full benefits of "sonship" until after we die. In the meantime, we live in a sinful world and will have our share of suffering. God uses some of that suffering to help us grow [as a parent helps a child develop discipline]. And we have what others don't—a sure sense of hope.)

8. **Look at verses 26 and 27. Have you ever tried to pray, but couldn't find the words? How did this feel?** (Note that God knows how we feel even when we can't express it, thanks to the intercession of the Holy Spirit.)

9. **Do verses 28-30 mean that if you wreck your parents' car, the insurance company will give them a better one? Explain.** (God understands and can bring good out of any situation—but we may not see or understand that good in this life. And God is the judge of what's good for us.) **Has God already brought good from a tough situation in your life? If so, how?**

10. **What's the worst thing you think could ever happen to you?** (Let students respond. Then read verses 31-39 and discuss God's unconditional, unbreakable love.) **What kind of music would make a good background for this passage? Why?**

This chapter contains some of God's most wonderful promises. Yet kids' feelings may not have caught up with these facts. The reproducible sheet, "Your Version," will have kids consider how much they've personally experienced the effects of some of these promises. Follow up by affirming two things: (1) If our feelings haven't caught up with the facts, that's not necessarily a reason to feel guilty; it's an opportunity to learn more about how trustworthy God is. (2) God's trustworthiness doesn't depend on our feelings, any more than a car's protective air bag depends on the driver's feelings. You may want to summarize how to become a Christian, since these promises are directed to "those who are in Christ Jesus."

Your Version

*H*ere are some statements from Romans 8. The real ones are first, after each number. But if one of the other versions of each statement matches your feelings more, put a check mark by it. If none of the versions of a statement matches your feelings, write in a version of your own.

1. "We hope for what we do not yet have, and wait for it patiently."

"We hope for what we do not yet have, but the waiting is killing us."

"We hope for the best, but really don't think things are going to work out."

Other:

_____

_____

2. "There is now no condemnation for those who are in Christ Jesus."

"There is less condemnation for those who are in Christ Jesus."

"I feel condemned even though I think I'm supposed to be in Christ Jesus."

Other:

_____

_____

3. "You did not receive a spirit that makes you a slave again to fear."

"You did not receive a spirit that makes you a slave again to fear, but you are afraid anyway."

"You do not have the Spirit's permission to be afraid, ever."

Other:

_____

_____

4. "We are God's children."

"We are God's children, but not His favorites."

"We are God's great-great-grandnephews, twice removed."

Other:

_____

_____

5. "Our present sufferings are not worth comparing with the glory that will be revealed in us."

"The glory that will be revealed in us is not worth comparing with our present sufferings."

"God does not care about our present sufferings, but only about His glory."

Other:

_____

_____

6. "The Spirit helps in our weakness."

"The Spirit helps other people in their weakness."

"The Spirit is too weak to help."

Other:

_____

_____

7. "In all things God works for the good of those who love Him."

"In some things God works for the good of those who love Him."

"In all things God works for His own good and forgets those who love Him."

Other:

_____

_____

8. "If God is for us, who can be against us?"

"If God is for the super-spiritual people, who can be against them?"

"With friends like God, who needs enemies?"

Other:

_____

_____

9. "I am convinced that [nothing] will be able to separate us from the love of God that is in Christ Jesus our Lord."

"I am convinced that some things might be able to separate us from the love of God that is in Christ Jesus our Lord."

"I would like to separate from the love of God that is in Christ Jesus our Lord."

Other:

_____

_____

ROMANS 9

Putting Pots In Their Place

Paul is deeply saddened that so many of his fellow Jews have been rejecting the Gospel. So he gives examples from Jewish history to show that God has frequently made some surprising choices about whom He would include or bless—as He has now also made salvation available to the Gentiles. The bottom line is that God's choices are up to Him.

Have a ventriloquism contest. Let kids find objects in the room that will act as their "puppets" (these could range from hymnals to fellow group members). See who can best "throw" his or her voice by appearing to make the "puppet" talk. The ventriloquists who move their mouths least as they talk should get the highest marks. For added challenge, require kids to use a lot of words that start with *B*—as in the phrase, "Rubber baby buggy bumpers." After the contest, explain that in this chapter Paul talks about how ridiculous it would be for one object—a pot—to talk back to its maker.

DATE I USED THIS SESSION _____ GROUP I USED IT WITH _____

NOTES FOR NEXT TIME_____

_____

_____

1. Can you think of two brothers or sisters who have opposite personalities? Why do you think they're so different?

2. Paul saw big differences among his Jewish "brothers." Some heard the good news about Jesus and embraced it. Others, however, felt no need for Jesus as Messiah. **How did Paul feel about the ones who rejected the Gospel** (vss. 1-3)? (He felt "great sorrow and unceasing anguish"—so much that he wished he could sacrifice his own relationship with Christ if it would somehow help all the others.)

3. Many Jewish people took pride in being "children of Abraham," but **what else did Paul say was necessary for them to find God's favor** (vss. 6-9)? (Abraham was singled out for his faith because he believed the promises of God. The Jewish people, rather than counting on their status as physical descendants of Abraham, also needed to reflect his personal faith. This would lead to believing that Jesus was the Messiah God had sent.)

4. If your parents are Christians but you aren't, what benefits should you expect from God? If you've received Christ, but no one else in your family has, how will that probably affect you? (Family members may influence a child in one way or another, but the ultimate decision of whether or not to believe is up to each individual.)

5. What's the point of the story of the children (vss. 10-16)? (Usually the oldest son got twice the inheritance of other children and the main blessing of the father. Yet God didn't always single out oldest children through which to pass His special blessing from generation to generation. Among others, He chose Isaac over Ishmael and Jacob over Esau. Was God unfair to do that? No. He's not bound by human tradition or expectation. In the same way, He could offer salvation to Gentiles as well as Jews.)

6. Why is Pharaoh (vss. 17, 18) a good example of someone resisting God? (He suffered all those plagues rather than let the Israelites go.) Was it fair for God to "harden" Pharaoh's heart so that would happen? (Paul's point is that

God has the right to do that—to choose when He will be merciful.)

7. **Look at verses 19-21. How do people today "talk back to God"? Why do they think they have that right? Does this mean we should never express our frustration to God?** (God cares about our pain, our doubts, and our questions, and it's good to express them [see David's psalms, for instance]. But it's not our place to spend a lifetime arguing with God that we should be something other than we are.)

8. **Paul backs up his point with more Old Testament passages** (vss. 22-29). **If you had been one of his Jewish readers, how might you have reacted?**

9. **What facts about Jesus are a "stumbling stone"** (vs. 32) **to people who might otherwise accept Him today?** (His teachings about sin and hell; His claim to be the only way to God; His commands about self-denial, etc.) **Is there anything about you that could cause non-Christians to "stumble" on their way to meeting Jesus?**

Most young people struggle with self-image and may feel that God has blessed others much more than themselves. The reproducible sheet, "Out of the Same Lump," helps them show what they think of themselves. When they finish, let volunteers share what they've done. Affirm kids by reminding them that God has created each of them differently—for a good reason. Ask: **What could you do for the Lord that others might find it hard or boring or scary to do?** Encourage anyone who is having a particularly rough time with self-esteem to talk to you later.

OUT OF THE SAME LUMP

"Shall what is formed say to him who formed it, 'Why did you make me like this?' Does not the potter have the right to make out of the same lump of clay some pottery for noble purposes and some for common use?"

(Romans 9:20, 21)

What kind of "pot" has God made you to be? Have you ever wanted to ask Him, "Hey, why did You make me like this?" Circle the pot on this page that's most like you. Or, if none of them are anything like you, draw your own pot to show how you feel about the way God has made you.

Coffeepot

People come to me when they want to be social, to have a good time. I have a lot of friends. I like to keep things bubbling.

Flowerpot

Others tend to get more attention than I do, even if I'm their main support. I'm not glamorous, but things might be a mess without me.

Crockpot

I'm the quiet, deliberate type. I take my time to get things done, but I do them right.

Teapot

Some people think I'm old-fashioned, or even wimpy. But I'm just as "hot" as anybody else, and I can make some noise when I feel like it.

Potpourri Pot

I like to change the atmosphere around me—for the better. Making a difference is important to me.

Soup Pot

I have a lot of different ingredients in me. Sometimes I feel all mixed up; sometimes I boil over.

Paint Pot

I'm a pretty colorful character. I'm always changing—feeling "blue" one day and "yellow" the next.

Stainless Steel Cooking Pot

I work hard and take a lot of heat. But I don't always get credit for it because—at least on the outside—I seem to hold up so well.

Crackpot

I make a lot of wisecracks. I try not to show it, but sometimes I feel a little broken inside.

Other

ROMANS 10

What Pretty Feet!

Paul continues his plea to Jewish people who have resisted the Gospel. Though they are zealous for righteousness, their efforts have been misdirected. He encourages them to instead confess Jesus as Lord and believe in His resurrection. Paul also quotes the Old Testament to honor those who proclaim the good news about Jesus to others.

(Needed: Prize)

Stage a "most beautiful toe" contest. Start at the "local beauty pageant" level, where each person decides which of his or her toes is most presentable. Then progress to "state pageants," where teams choose their most beautiful representative toe. Finally, the "state" winners compete in the "nationals" (in front of the whole group). Make the "national pageant" as elaborate or as simple as you like, and award a prize to the winner. Then explain that in this chapter Paul praises the "beautiful feet" of those who spread the good news about Jesus.

DATE I USED THIS SESSION _____ GROUP I USED IT WITH _____

NOTES FOR NEXT TIME _____

_____

_____

1. Suppose you have one wish—and it has to be something for your family. What would you wish for?

2. What was Paul's #1 wish for his "brothers," the Jewish people (vs. 1)? (He wanted them to accept the truth that Jesus was their Savior so they could be saved from their sins.)

3. How "religious" would you say the Jews were (vs. 2)? (Very. Yet even though they worked hard and took their religion very seriously, their zeal was in vain since they refused to believe that Jesus was the Messiah.)

4. The Jews were right to try to follow the Law, but what crucial point were they missing (vss. 3, 4)? (The Law pointed to Jesus, who provides righteousness to whoever believes—not just to those who follow established rituals and traditions.)

5. What's the most "heroic" Old Testament story you can think of? (Examples: David and Goliath, the three men in the fiery furnace, etc.) **Paul explains that great acts of courage aren't a requirement for righteousness (vss. 5, 7). What *is* required (vss. 8-10)?** (To confess that Jesus is Lord and truly believe in His resurrection from the dead. The same is required of Gentiles [vss. 11-13].)

6. Look at verses 14 and 15. Why did Paul talk about "beautiful feet"? (The "beautiful feet" quote refers to Isaiah 52:7, where the prophet describes those who would proclaim that Israel was no longer in exile. Similarly, the Gospel message is one of freedom and release from the captivity of sin.)

7. What had been the problem in the past when God had tried to communicate with the nation of Israel (vss. 16-21)? (Paul calls the Israelites "a disobedient and obstinate people." They had frequently resisted what they knew to be God's will for them in order to accommodate their own selfish interests.) **Do you think this describes non-Christians today, too? How about Christians? Why or why not?**

8. What percentage of people your age would you estimate don't know the truth about Jesus or how to become a Christian? What percentage do you think know the facts, but don't understand them? How many would you say know and understand, but just don't want to make any kind of commitment?

The reproducible sheet, "Talk Back," will help kids consider and discuss their attitudes about sharing their faith. After everyone has completed the sheet, talk about it. Then ask: **If you wanted to tell a friend about Christ, what examples could you give from your own life to "back up" Romans 10:11?** If time allows, let volunteers practice talking naturally about what Jesus means to them. This doesn't even have to be in a "witnessing" context. Many Christian kids are so unused to talking about anything "spiritual" outside of church that they need help to see that it's possible to talk about God without sounding—or being—phony.

Talk Back

For each of these verses, check the response that comes closest to yours—or write in another.

"How, then, can they call on the one they have not believed in? And how can they believe in the one of whom they have not heard? And how can they hear without someone preaching to them? And how can they preach unless they are sent? As it is written, 'How beautiful are the feet of those who bring good news!'" (Romans 10:14, 15)

❏ I give up. How can they?
❏ This is just for paid professionals like preachers and missionaries (whew).
❏ Typical Bible quote—just trying to make me feel guilty.
❏ And how can I do the "preaching" without making a fool of myself?
❏ I've tried sharing my faith, and nobody thought my "feet" were very beautiful.
❏ I want to bring my friends the Good News, but I don't know how.
❏ Other _____

"... If you confess with your mouth, 'Jesus is Lord,' and believe in your heart that God raised him from the dead, you will be saved" (Romans 10:9).

❏ This is too simple. It can't be right.
❏ Why open your mouth? Isn't it enough to just believe?
❏ I haven't done this myself yet.
❏ If I put that in my own words, maybe I could tell somebody that.
❏ Other

_____

"As the Scripture says, 'Anyone who trusts in him will never be put to shame'" (Romans 10:11).

❏ I wouldn't mind telling a friend this, because it's been true for me.
❏ This hasn't been my experience.
❏ I'm afraid *I'd* be put to shame if I tried to tell anybody this.
❏ Other _____

"... Everyone who calls on the name of the Lord will be saved" (Romans 10:13).

❏ Some of the people I know don't deserve to be saved.
❏ You mean that's all I have to get them to do?
❏ Maybe there will be more people in heaven than I thought.
❏ Other

_____

Your Jewish Roots

Paul explains that salvation's availability to Gentiles doesn't mean God has rejected the Jewish people. In fact, the Gentiles' access to God can be an attention-getter for many of the Jewish people. As they become less hardened to the message of the Gospel, God will provide salvation for them, too.

(Needed: Two kinds of cereal; two paper grocery bags; stopwatch; team prize)

Before the session, get two kinds of cereal that are similar in shape, but slightly different (such as Spoon Size Shredded Wheat and Wheat Chex). Pour a lot of one kind and just one piece of the other kind into a grocery bag. Do the same with another bag. When the session starts, form teams. Each team should line up at a bag. The first member of each team will have five seconds to try to find the "odd" piece of cereal in his or her team's bag (by touch only; no looking). If the first person doesn't succeed, the next person tries. Keep time with a stopwatch and call out, "Switch!" at five-second intervals. The first team to find its "odd" piece of cereal wins. Give the winners a prize. Use this "needle in a haystack" game to illustrate the idea of the "remnant" of Israel discussed in this chapter.

DATE I USED THIS SESSION _____ GROUP I USED IT WITH _____

NOTES FOR NEXT TIME _____

_____

_____

1. When was the last time you felt really "left out" of something? Did you feel mostly angry, lonely, sad, rejected, or something else?

2. Some of the Jewish people were feeling left out as Christianity began to spread. Why? (They had always felt special to God—and they were. But now they saw many Gentiles, people they felt were unclean and not worthy of God's love, becoming Christians and receiving God's favor. Yet the Jewish people were not being rejected by God [vss. 1, 2].)

3. Paul tried to explain that the Jewish people had frequently felt more alone than they actually were (vss. 2-4). Have you ever felt alone, but later discovered that someone was thinking of you or remembered that God was with you? When?

4. While most of the Hebrew people may have turned their backs on God, a "remnant" of them were still faithful. As Paul wrote to the Romans, who composed the "remnant" of Israel (vss. 5-10)? (The ones who realized that they were acceptable to God because of His grace—not because of their own works.)

5. Do you sometimes feel alone (as a Christian) at school or elsewhere? Do you think God has a "remnant" of people in your school who believe as you do? If so, how might you and these other people discover and encourage each other?

6. Now that salvation had come to the Gentiles, was it too late for Jewish people (vss. 11, 12)? **Explain.** (Not at all. They had "stumbled," but the envy they felt toward the Gentiles should have motivated them to take action.)

7. Look at verses 13-24, addressed to Gentiles. What advice did Paul give them that applies today as well (vss. 13-24)? (Not to be arrogant about being "grafted" onto the "tree" of God's grace.) Have you ever heard a non-Jewish person express a disrespectful view of Jewish people? Have you heard a Christian do that? Based on verse 18, how do you think Paul would react?

8. **What was Paul predicting for the Jewish people** (vss. 25-32)**?** (That they would receive God's mercy and be saved, apparently as a result of coming to accept Jesus as the Messiah.)

9. **Based on verses 33-36, do you think Paul understood God?** (He didn't claim to. The better we get to know God, the more we realize how little we really understand.) **What about God do you find most "unsearchable"?**

Paul makes it clear in this chapter that Gentiles have no reason to feel superior to Jews. Yet anti-Semitic comments are all too common among professing Christians. Give each group member a copy of the reproducible sheet, "Anti-Anti." Kids should read the instructions and myths, then fill in the "my feelings" sections individually. Form four teams to look up the Bible passages and paraphrase answers to the statements (one statement per team). Then discuss. Follow up by asking: **If you were a Jewish person who didn't accept the idea that Jesus is the Messiah, how would you feel about Christians? What kinds of statements about Jewish people might keep them from considering Christ? What changes might you need to make in the way you relate to and talk about Jewish people?** (Note: If yours is a Messianic Jewish congregation, discuss ways in which you could help Gentile Christians become more sensitive to Jewish people).

Anti-Anti

anti-Semitism (ant-eye-SEM-uh-tiz-um): hostility toward or discrimination against Jews as a religious or racial group [Webster's New Collegiate Dictionary].

Jewish people have been targets of discrimination—and much worse—for thousands of years. And people who claim to be Christians have done too much of the discriminating. Here are four statements some have made about Jewish people. Using the facts, how could you reply to each myth? Be sure to put each answer in your own words.

MYTH: "The Jews are to blame for killing Christ."
MY FEELINGS ABOUT IT: _____
FACTS: John 3:16; Galatians 1:3, 4; John 19:8-11, 16; Luke 23:34

_____

_____

MYTH: "God loves Christians, not Jews."
MY FEELINGS ABOUT IT: _____
FACTS: Romans 11:1, 2; Psalm 136; Matthew 23:37-39

_____

_____

MYTH: "Jews and Christians have nothing in common."
MY FEELINGS ABOUT IT: _____
FACTS: John 4:19-24; Romans 9:1-5; I Corinthians 12:12, 13

_____

_____

MYTH: "The Jews have rejected Jesus, so Christians should reject them."
MY FEELINGS ABOUT IT: _____
FACTS: Romans 11:17-21; 15:27

_____

_____

ROMANS 12

Altar Egos

In response to God's gift of salvation, we should become "living sacrifices" in service to Him. This job requires humility, willingness to work with other Christians, love, patience, and peacemaking—toward enemies as well as friends.

(Needed: Index card with questions on it)

Take a group vote to select a sports figure, musician, movie star, or other celebrity who's held in high regard. Have a volunteer play the role of that person. Say: **Suppose** [name of celebrity] **is looking for an assistant to travel with him** [or her]**, run errands, and help out with personal appearances. You're interviewing for that job.** Have your volunteer conduct a "group interview," asking questions of group members to see who is most willing to serve. Interview questions (which you should copy onto an index card before the session) might include "Why do you want this job?" "How do you feel about 'waiting on' someone else?" "Would you be willing to set aside your own plans if I suddenly needed you?" "What would you hope to learn from me?" Let the volunteer pick the person with the best "servant" attitude. As you begin your discussion about "living sacrifices," explain that this is the attitude we need to develop toward God.

DATE I USED THIS SESSION _____ GROUP I USED IT WITH _____

NOTES FOR NEXT TIME _____

_____

_____

1. There's a myth that cats have nine lives. What if you had the option to have nine lives? Would you want it, even if it meant dying nine times? Explain.

2. Do you think it's harder to die for someone, or to live for that person? In other words, would it be more difficult to make a onetime, final sacrifice, or to spend a lifetime doing whatever that person asked of you?

3. Paul challenges us to become "living sacrifices" (vs. 1) because God has forgiven our sins and made us His own. Somebody has joked that living sacrifices are hard to manage, since they keep crawling off the altar. What do you think that means? (Even if we want to serve God faithfully, we'll always struggle in this life with selfish desires that conflict with God's will.)

4. What are some "pattern[s] of this world" (vs. 2) that you think it's OK to "conform" to? What are some that you think God doesn't like?

5. How can you renew your mind (vs. 2)? Why would you want to? (It's a lifelong process of rising above "normal" worldly standards and tuning in to what God wants. It happens as you feed your mind on God's instructions, by studying the Bible and learning to be sensitive to the Holy Spirit. With your "old" mind, God's will is less clear, and you stay stuck in the patterns of those around you.)

6. God wants us to "play our positions" in the church (vss. 3-8). Which of the gifts listed here sounds most interesting to you? Which of these activities have you tried? Which do you think you might be "gifted" to do?

7. Do you think more teenagers think of themselves more highly than they should (vs. 3), or less highly?

8. How have you seen people under the age of twenty-one show each of the following (from verses 9-16)? What was the result in each case?

- **Sincere love**
- **Hating what is evil**
- **Zeal for spiritual things**
- **Patience in affliction**
- **Practicing hospitality**
- **Lack of conceit**
- **Lack of pride**
- **Associating with people of low position**
- **Devotion to one another in brotherly love**

- **Honoring others above oneself**
- **Being joyful in hope**
- **Faithfulness in prayer**
- **Sharing with those in need**
- **Blessing one's persecutors**
- **Empathy for others' emotions**

9. When was the last time you refused to repay "evil for evil" (vs. 17)? Why did you do it?

10. How could you "overcome evil with good" (vss. 18-21) **if the evil was (a) unfair treatment by a teacher; (b) gang influence in your neighborhood?**

The reproducible sheet, "Roger's Reaction," will help make sure that kids understand the "real world" meaning of several of Paul's commands in this chapter. When they finish, discuss their "corrections." Then ask: **Which of the commands in this chapter do you wish you could "correct"—because you'd rather not do them?** Challenge each person to choose just one of the commands in the chapter, come up with a way to obey it during the next 24 hours, and share that plan with a partner.

Roger's Reaction

*T*he following memo contains some misunderstandings of what Paul was trying to say in this chapter. Can you correct them in the margins?

TO: **The Apostle Paul**
FROM: **Roger Roman**
SUBJECT: **Romans 12**

I have received your recent letter, and am concerned over your instructions. As I understand it, you want me to:

• Sacrifice myself by climbing onto an altar and setting myself on fire (vs. 1). I fail to see the point of this. I also think it violates the fire marshal's code for my apartment building.

• Get a brain transplant (vs. 2). I have been unable to find a physician who knows how to perform this operation. My insurance company also refuses to cover the expense.

• Think of myself as worthless (vs. 3) and let others treat me like dirt (vs. 10). I believe this would be bad for my self-image, not to mention my white slacks.

• Practice in a hospital (vs. 13). I assume you want me to practice as a surgeon, a job for which I have no training. Perhaps it's your intention that I practice there in order to learn to do brain transplants (see second point above).

• Please everyone at once (vs. 17). Since people disagree with each other about what is right, this is quite impossible. Or do you mean that I should follow majority opinion, whatever it happens to be?

• Pile burning coals on the heads of my enemies (vs. 20). Now, this is an excellent idea. My only question is this: Is actual coal required, or are the charcoal briquets from my backyard barbecue acceptable?

Thank you for your prompt attention to this matter. Until I hear from you, I will continue to obey the command to "do nothing" (John 15:5).

ROMANS 13

Under Their Thumbs

A life devoted to God includes submitting to human governing authorities, because they're part of God's plan for order in the world. Generally speaking, when we cause no trouble for them, we should have nothing to fear. We should not only pay our taxes and meet our obligations, but respect our leaders as well. Paul also reminds us to love our neighbors as ourselves because the time of Jesus' return is approaching.

(Needed: A dozen editorial cartoons; two envelopes; team prize [optional])

Before the session, cut a dozen political cartoons from newspapers. All should have captions. Cut off the captions; put half the cartoons and their captions in one envelope, and half in another. When the session begins, form two teams. Give each team an envelope. See which team can match its cartoons and captions first. Award a prize to the winners if you like. Then ask: **What points are these cartoons trying to make? Do you think any of them go too far in making fun of people? On a scale of 1 to 10 (10 highest), how much do you respect most of our country's leaders? Why?**

DATE I USED THIS SESSION _____ GROUP I USED IT WITH _____

NOTES FOR NEXT TIME_____

_____

_____

1. Think of a teacher you just couldn't (or can't) seem to get along with. What was (or is) the problem?

2. What words or phrases come to mind when you hear each of the following: **(a) police officer; (b) politician; (c) parent; (d) president?**

3. Look at verse 1. What do you think this means for comedians who make jokes about national leaders? For kids who call their parents by their first names? For kids who have negative nicknames for teachers they don't like? (This may depend on how the jokes, first names, and nicknames are meant and how they're taken by their "targets." Even beneath "acceptable" jokes and informality, we need to maintain sincere respect for each person in authority.)

4. Why did Paul even care how we treat those in authority? How could he know how badly they might treat us (vs. 2)? (Paul knew that authorities are part of God's plan for maintaining order in the world. Yet he lived under the rule of some of the worst of the Roman emperors. He knew that human leaders are far from perfect.)

5. Does this mean we shouldn't try to vote bad leaders out of office, or find better jobs when a boss is unfair? Explain. (Our political system provides ways to change government without rebelling [vs. 3]; Paul's generally didn't. In Paul's day some people could change jobs without rebelling, but slaves usually couldn't. Many of us have more options today, but our attitudes of respect should be the same—no matter who wins an election, and no matter whether we can afford to quit a job or not.)

6. Assuming you can't change the situation, what's the best way to deal with a "bad" teacher or boss (vss. 2-5)? (By behaving ourselves we'll avoid giving such people a reason to get on our cases.)

7. What attitudes about taxes and respecting government officials (vss. 6, 7) do you think you've picked up from your parents? Where else have your attitudes come from?

8. Based on verses 8-10, what should it mean when you say "I love you" to a girlfriend or boyfriend? To a parent? To God?

9. Look at verses 11 and 12. What are some of the night-time activities that take place among teenagers that they might be too afraid or ashamed to do during the day? (Drinking; sexual activity; theft, etc.) Which of these things should we "put aside"?

10. When Christ returns, it will be "daytime" again (vss. 12-14). What are some of the things you'll be glad to leave behind when that time comes?

11. What do you think it means to "clothe yourselves with the Lord Jesus Christ" (vs. 14)? (One possibility: Become more like Him in our actions as well as in our thoughts.)

Have kids complete the sentences on the reproducible sheet, "Universal Remote." Discuss their answers as much as they're willing. If possible, fill out one of the sheets yourself and share some answers as an example. Then spend some time in silent prayer, giving kids a chance to talk to God about the thoughts they expressed on the sheet.

UNIVERSAL REMOTE

Don't look now, but Christ is returning soon. Between now and then, Paul says, we've got a lot of growing up to do—in the way we feel about authorities, in the way we show love to other people, and in our attitudes toward things like sex, alcohol, and partying.

If you're going to "clothe your[self] with the Lord Jesus Christ, and . . . not think about how to gratify the desires of the sinful nature," where should you start? Complete the sentences to show how you could start getting this part of your life under "control."

POWER
I need to ask God to help me overcome . . .

_____

REWIND
I need to go "back to the beginning" and start fresh by . . .

_____

STOP
I need to quit . . .

_____

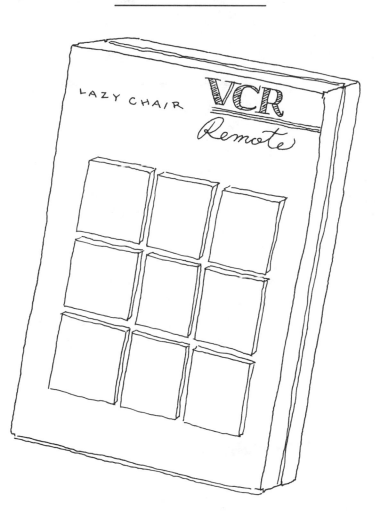

PLAY
I need to stop putting off . . .

_____

PAUSE
I need to rest because . . .

_____

SEARCH
I need to find out what God wants me to do about . . .

_____

VOLUME
I need to speak up more when other people . . .

_____

FAST FORWARD
I need to plan ahead for . . .

_____

CHANGE CHANNELS
I need to concentrate more on . . .

_____

PROGRAM
I need to "program" my mind with stuff like . . .

_____

RECORD
I need to remember or memorize . . .

_____

EJECT
I need to get rid of . . .

_____

Walking on Eggs

One sign of maturity is putting up with people who we think aren't as mature as we are. When other Christians deny themselves things that we feel are OK, we should allow them that right, without judging them. We should be concerned with our *own* obedience to God. It's not worth damaging or destroying a relationship just so that we can promote our list of—or lack of—rules.

(Needed: Two pairs of thick gloves; two boxes of toothpicks; prizes [optional])

Form two teams. Have each team choose a representative; the other team members will cheer him or her on. Each representative must put on a pair of thick gloves. Dump the contents of a box of toothpicks in front of each representative. Wearing the gloves, he or she must spell the word *SENSITIVITY* using the toothpicks. Whoever finishes first is the winner. Award team prizes if you like. Then point out that this chapter talks about the need for believers to be sensitive to each other's views of what's OK for Christians to do. Just as the gloves made it harder to be "sensitive" enough to manipulate the toothpicks, our lack of sensitivity can cause us to offend each other.

DATE I USED THIS SESSION _____ GROUP I USED IT WITH _____

NOTES FOR NEXT TIME _____

_____

_____

1. Were you ever so sick that you could barely move—and other people had to bring you everything you needed? How did you feel toward these people? How do you think they felt toward you?

2. When people become Christians, they're often "weak" spiritually and need help from those who are stronger. How have you been helped by a more experienced Christian to grow stronger in your faith?

3. What are you free to do now that you weren't free to do ten years ago? (Let kids respond.) Spiritual maturity provides freedom to do things that may *seem* wrong to others. For example, what were some of the issues Paul mentions (vss. 1-8)? (Some people were probably holding to the traditional Jewish dietary restrictions, while others claimed the newly given freedom to eat anything [Acts 10:9-16]. Some still observed the "holy" days they always had; others tried to devote every day to God.)

4. Which of these actions were sinful? (None of them—so Paul said people should have the freedom to do them or not.)

5. What issue was more important than any of these controversies (vss. 1, 9-11)? (Tolerating the less developed faith of another without passing judgment is needed for Christian unity.)

6. Do you think this means we should overlook the *sins* of fellow Christians? (No. Other passages [such as James 5:19, 20] deal with this. But when sin is not an issue, we should give others some latitude in their personal practices.)

7. How would you feel about a member of our group who did the following: (a) refused to laugh at jokes or play games "because there are people starving in the world"; (b) wouldn't go to a Christian rock concert "because rock is the devil's music"; (c) refused to eat any meat, "because animals are God's creatures too, and we shouldn't kill them"? What do you think Paul's advice in these cases would be?

8. When we're tempted to judge others, what should we remember (vs. 12)? (Each individual will be accountable to God for his or her own actions. It's usually a full-time job to obey God ourselves, much less trying to monitor others.)

9. Have the actions of another Christian ever caused you to "stumble" (vs. 13)? If so, how?

10. What was Paul's personal opinion about the food issue (vs. 14-18)? How did he try to get others to agree with it (vss. 19-23)? (He felt it was OK to eat any kind of food. But he focused on spiritual issues like righteousness, peace, and joy—and unity among Christians. Instead of trying to convince others on the food issue, he voluntarily limited his own actions to those that would be accepted by his "weaker" fellow Christians.)

11. If you think something is wrong and other Christians don't, should you do it anyway? Why or why not? (See verse 23. If you deliberately did something you thought was wrong, you'd be sinning. For example, if you thought the speed limit was 35 and decided to disregard it and go 55, you'd be showing a lawless attitude. Still, we should be open to learning more about what the Bible says about right and wrong and having our attitudes changed.)

In order to not offend other Christians, we first need to know what's offensive to them. Many kids haven't thought much about the beliefs of Christians outside their own church (or even those *in* it). Have group members complete the reproducible sheet, "Non-Smoking Section." Discuss the results, adding comments that reflect your own views and those of your church if you like. Then have each person single out one thing he or she feels free to do that might bother others. **How can you keep from offending people with this behavior? What do you think Jesus would do?**

NON-SMOKING SECTION

Christians don't always see eye to eye. Here's a list of activities, and four boxes. Put each activity in the box(es) where you think it belongs.

I THINK THESE THINGS ARE OK, BUT SOME CHRISTIANS DON'T	I THINK ALL CHRISTIANS BELIEVE THESE THINGS ARE OK
I THINK ALL CHRISTIANS BELIEVE THESE THINGS ARE WRONG	**SOME PEOPLE THINK THESE THINGS ARE OK, BUT I DON'T**

Wearing casual clothes to church
Wearing jewelry
Long hair on guys
Abortion
Comic books
Joining the army
Interracial dating
Girls wearing pants
Sex before marriage
Bowling
Believing in evolution
Homosexual feelings
Going to the store on Sunday

Homosexual acts
Watching MTV
Rock music
Dancing
Christian rock music
Smoking cigarettes
Mild profanity
Smoking marijuana
All movies
Adults who drink without getting drunk
R-rated movies
Guys and girls swimming together
NC-17 movies

Underage drinking
Nintendo games
Skipping church every once in a while
Violent TV shows
Alcoholism
Playing cards
Playing the lottery
Not saying grace at meals
Casino gambling
Drawing nudes in art class
Not having regular personal devotions
Dating non-Christians

Let's Stay Together

We need to be patient with the failings of other Christians, build them up, and develop a Christlike spirit of servanthood. The goal: unity among believers. As Paul starts winding up this letter, he again explains his work among the Gentiles and his hope that he can soon visit Rome.

(Needed: Two kids in sweat suits; padding)

Before the session, get two kids to dress in sweat suits and to stuff padding (paper towels, foam rubber, etc.) in their clothing to make themselves look like bodybuilders. Have them practice the skit on the reproducible sheet, "The Big Buildup." Encourage them to sound as much like Arnold Schwartzenegger as they can, in the style of the old "Hans and Franz" sketches on TV's *Saturday Night Live*. When the session starts, have your two actors perform the skit. Then ask the group: **Do you feel "built up" now? Why not? What does it mean to "build each other up"?** Point out that negative comments like those of the skit characters do anything but build people up. That kind of "buildup" is addressed in this chapter.

DATE I USED THIS SESSION _____ GROUP I USED IT WITH _____

NOTES FOR NEXT TIME_____

_____

_____

1. Suppose a friend of yours is a new Christian. He or she asks you to go with him or her to a Christian concert—to hear an artist whose music you feel is "lame." What do you tell your friend? Why?

2. What do you think Paul would have done in the same situation (vss. 1, 2)? (He probably would have gone. If the concert benefits a "weaker" friend, we probably shouldn't discourage the person.)

3. If Jesus had been mainly interested in pleasing Himself (vss. 3, 4), how might your life be different today?

4. How can you tell when a group of Christians have a spirit of unity (vss. 5, 6)? Does our group have it? Does our church have it? Explain.

5. Have you ever been in a group of Christians who were singing and felt you were glorifying God "with one heart and mouth"? If this is unusual, why do you think that is?

6. On a scale of 1 to 100 percent, how completely do you think Christ accepts you (vs. 7)? On the same scale, how completely do you accept most other people (on average)?

7. If God had not extended His offer of salvation to Gentiles as well as Jews (vss. 7-13), what do you think your view of God would be today?

8. Let's say this group loses its leader, and there's no replacement. How long could you "instruct one another" (vs. 14) before running out of things to say? An hour? A month? A year? Why?

9. Look at verses 17-22. Paul wanted to carry the Gospel to people who had never heard it. How far would you have to go to find people who don't know that they need to receive Christ? (Probably not far. Even in our culture there are many people who know nothing about the Bible—and many who know a little about the Bible have only a vague idea of who Jesus is.) Can you describe how to become a Christian without using words like "saved," "sin," and "repent"? Give it a try right now.

10. Where did Paul want to go next (vss. 23-29)? (He wanted to visit with the Romans on his way to Spain.) **If you could pick any place in the world to share your faith, where would it be? Why?**

11. Paul asked for prayer. **Do you ever ask anyone to pray for you? Why or why not? How could our group pray for you this week?**

(Needed: Accompaniment for singing; songbooks [optional])

Practice glorifying God "with one heart and mouth" by singing together. Instead of just launching into a bunch of songs, however, take time to go over the lyrics of each song before singing. Make sure kids understand the lyrics, and that the group agrees on the truth of each song. If possible, have kids sit closer together than usual to encourage a feeling of unity.

THE BIG BUILDUP

Characters: Huntz and Fruntz, two Austrian bodybuilders

HUNTZ: Hello. I am Huntz.

FRUNTZ: And I am Fruntz. And we are here to . . .

BOTH: Build . . . *(they clap once)* you up! *(They flex their muscles, trying to be impressive.)*

HUNTZ: All right, all you little girly-men and girly-girls. You are so weak that you make me sick to my stomach.

FRUNTZ: You are all so weak you make me think that I could lift you with my little finger and put you inside a sausage roll and toss you into the dumpster behind my grandmother's bratwurst factory.

HUNTZ: You probably all wear frilly little pants that do not even come down to your knees.

FRUNTZ: And that is why we are here to . . .

BOTH: Build . . . *(they clap once)* you up! *(They flex their muscles again.)*

HUNTZ: All right, Fruntz. Let us tell these little wimpy-schnitzels how they can have handsomely sculpted bodies like our own.

FRUNTZ: You mean these massively muscled masterpieces which look as if they had been chiseled from huge chunks of granite?

HUNTZ: Yah. But these crying jellyfish are so weak that I do not think they could even lift one pound of sauerkraut.

FRUNTZ: That's right. I have never seen such weakness. It makes me want to hit my head with a barbell until my brains come out.

HUNTZ: Yah. They could never have the brawny strength of our perfectly formed physiques. *(They flex their muscles again.)*

FRUNTZ: Perhaps they should place bonnets on their heads and suck their thumbs like the little baby-persons they are.

HUNTZ: Why don't you all do that? And wear some diapers as part of the bargain.

FRUNTZ: Well, I see our time is gone for today.

HUNTZ: That's OK, because these squealy worm-babies will have to be drinking their bottles soon.

FRUNTZ: So if you all want to have amazingly powerful strength like ours, you can forget it.

HUNTZ: And remember, we are here to . . .

BOTH: Build . . . *(they clap once)* you up! *(They flex their muscles as they exit.)*

ROMANS 16

And Say Hello to . . .

As Paul closes his message to the Romans, he sends greetings to the people he knows, and introduces them to Phoebe (probably the person delivering his letter). He also gives a final warning to stay away from those who hinder other people's spiritual growth.

(Needed: Team prize [optional])

Form teams. Give each team a copy of the reproducible sheet, "Where in the World Is San Diego?" The first team to figure out where all four postcards were sent from, based on the hints in the messages, wins. (Or, after five minutes, the team with the most correct answers wins.) (Answers: [1] Pisa, Italy; [2] Hamburg, Germany; [3] Boise, Idaho; [4] St. Petersburg, Russia.) Use this activity to lead into the idea of sending greetings, something Paul did a lot of in this chapter.

DATE I USED THIS SESSION _____ GROUP I USED IT WITH _____

NOTES FOR NEXT TIME _____

_____

_____

1. Has anyone ever "paved the way" for you by setting up a blind date or a job interview, or some other introduction? What was the result? How might things have gone differently without the "help"?

2. Paul introduced his Roman readers to Phoebe (probably the person who would carry the letter to them). Some people have accused Paul of teaching elsewhere that women aren't "equal" to men. Based on what he says about Phoebe, do you think he thought less of women than he did of men (vs. 2)? (Paul had the highest regard for Phoebe, as he did for many women he worked with—including several he will mention later in this chapter.)

3. Paul never overlooked the people who helped him in his work for the Lord. What Christians could you thank for being like those Paul mentions in verses 3-16:

- Who make sacrifices for you?
- Who work hard on your behalf?
- Who have suffered with you?
- Whom you love?
- Who are good friends?
- Who are like a mother to you?

4. According to verses 17 and 18, who should we watch out for? How should we respond to such people? (We should stay away from those who cause divisions among Christians and who hinder our spiritual growth.) Is this your responsibility, or should you leave it to your church leaders? Explain.

5. How can you be "wise about what is good" (vs. 19)? (Right actions aren't easy or automatic. We need to work on what we know will honor God—through prayer, Bible study, obeying authority, and other spiritual disciplines.)

6. How can you be "innocent about what is evil"? (Some kids try everything "just to see what it's like." It's better to be completely removed [innocent] from the "line of fire" of temptations like drug use, sexual activity, shoplifting, etc.)

7. **Even as Paul was saying his "last good-byes" to the Romans, how did he honor God** (vss. 20, 25-27)**?** (He reminded his readers of God's ultimate victory over Satan, His power, His revelation of Himself, and His wisdom.)

8. **How do people today mention God in their greetings or departures?** ("Good-bye" is actually a contraction of "God be with you," but most people aren't aware of that. We may say an occasional "God bless you" as we say good-bye, but most of us aren't nearly as conscientious about focusing on God as Paul was.)

(Needed: Letter-writing supplies)

Paul knew personal greetings were important. Ask kids to list people they haven't kept in touch with lately—but who might be encouraged by a note. When all have compiled their lists, give them an opportunity to follow up by writing notes. If possible, provide an assortment of greeting cards, stationery, postcards, stamps, and envelopes. If kids have listed some of the same people (such as a former group member who moved out of town), have one person write the letter and let everyone else sign it. Or bring a speaker phone and have a group conversation.

WHERE IN THE WORLD IS SAN DIEGO?

Can you figure out what cities these postcards were sent from?

GREETINGS FROM SAN DIEGO!

Dear Carmen,
It's great here in the land of canals and ceilings. This city reminds me of a food teenagers like to eat. It towers over the other places I've been, and I'm leaning toward staying here another week.

Love,
Bernie

Hi!
This city sounds like a derby, but not the Kentucky kind. I was sure I'd find a lot of fast food places here selling 100 percent beef, but I guess not. Lots of sauerbraten, though!

Yours truly,
Alice

Dear Sue,
I'd, uh, hoped to see boys here—lots of 'em. I haven't, though. The sun has been baking me, so I've got quite a tan. I mashed my finger in a car door the other day, but things have been pleasant otherwise.

Your friend,
Charette

Hello, Larry!
Boy, did I goof! I thought I was headed for a city in Florida, but it's colder here. You might say that disciple, Simon, owns this place. The first part looks like a street, but it's holier than thou.

Best wishes,
Joey